THE FUNCTIONS OF THE HUMAN NERVOUS SYSTEM

BIOLOGY BOOKS FOR KIDS

Children's Biology Books

Speedy Publishing LLC

40 E. Main St. #1156

Newark, DE 19711

www.speedypublishing.com

Our nervous system is only one of 11 systems that makes up the human body. It consists of the brain, the spinal cord, and a network of nerves covering the entire body. In this book, you will be learning about the nervous system and how it works inside our bodies.

THE NERVOUS SYSTEM

Along with the nervous system, different parts of the human body are able to communicate which allows the brain to be in control over what goes on. The brain would mush without the assistance of it. It would not know what was occurring in the world outside and would not be able to control the body.

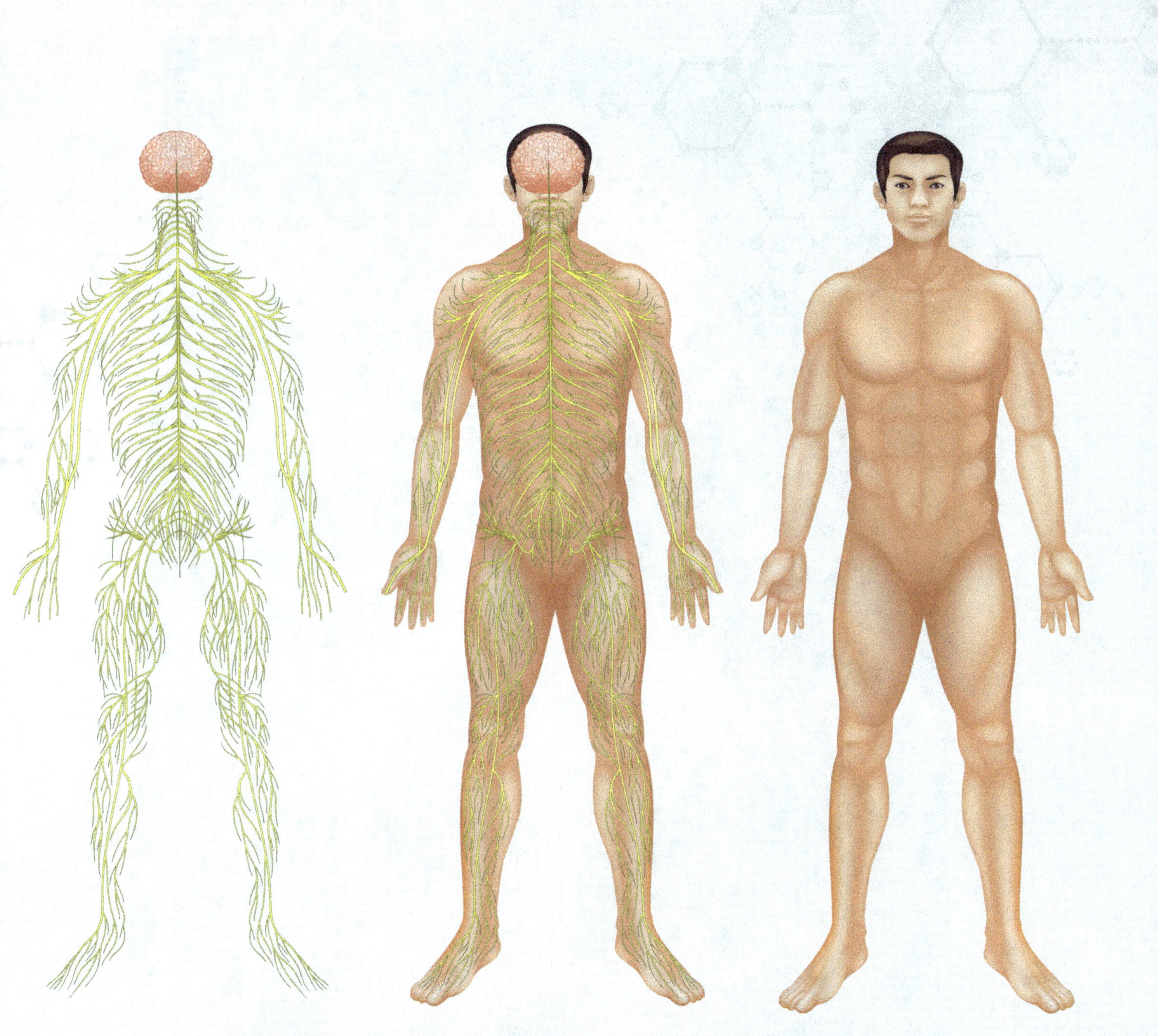

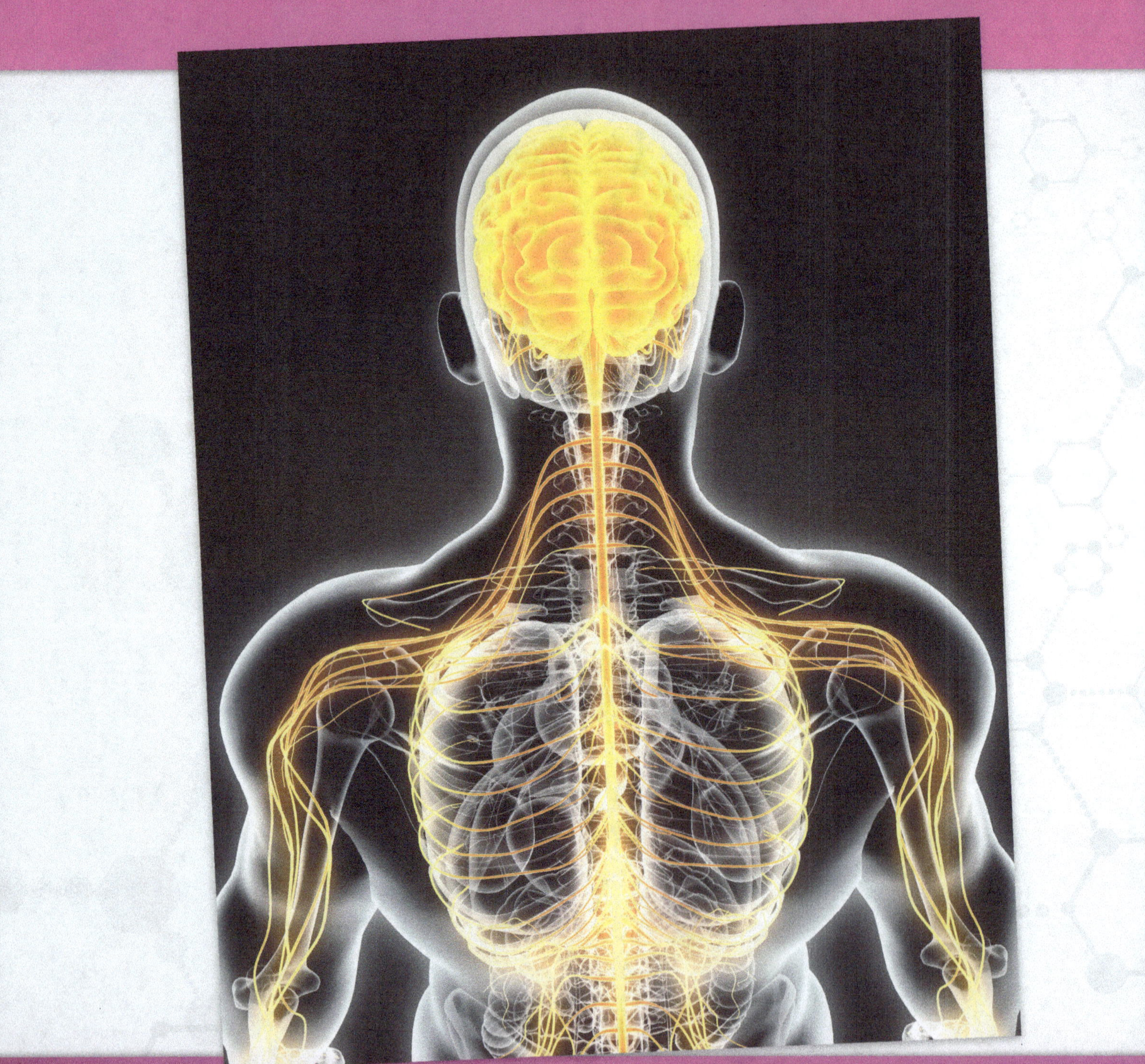

Along with the spinal cord, the brain makes up what is known as the central nervous system. The remaining nerves combined are referred to as the peripheral nervous system.

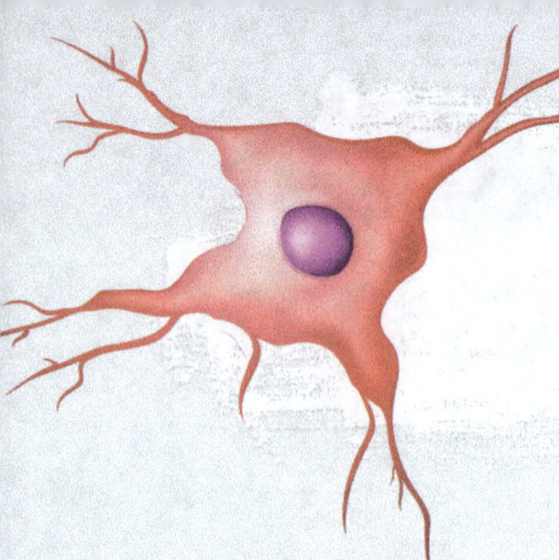

THE PERIPHERAL NERVOUS SYSTEM

Nerves resemble wires carrying signals that communicate throughout our body. There is a collection of nerve fibers inside each nerve, some of them being very long, including the ones going from your spinal cord to your feet. The nerve cells are known as neurons.

Neurons

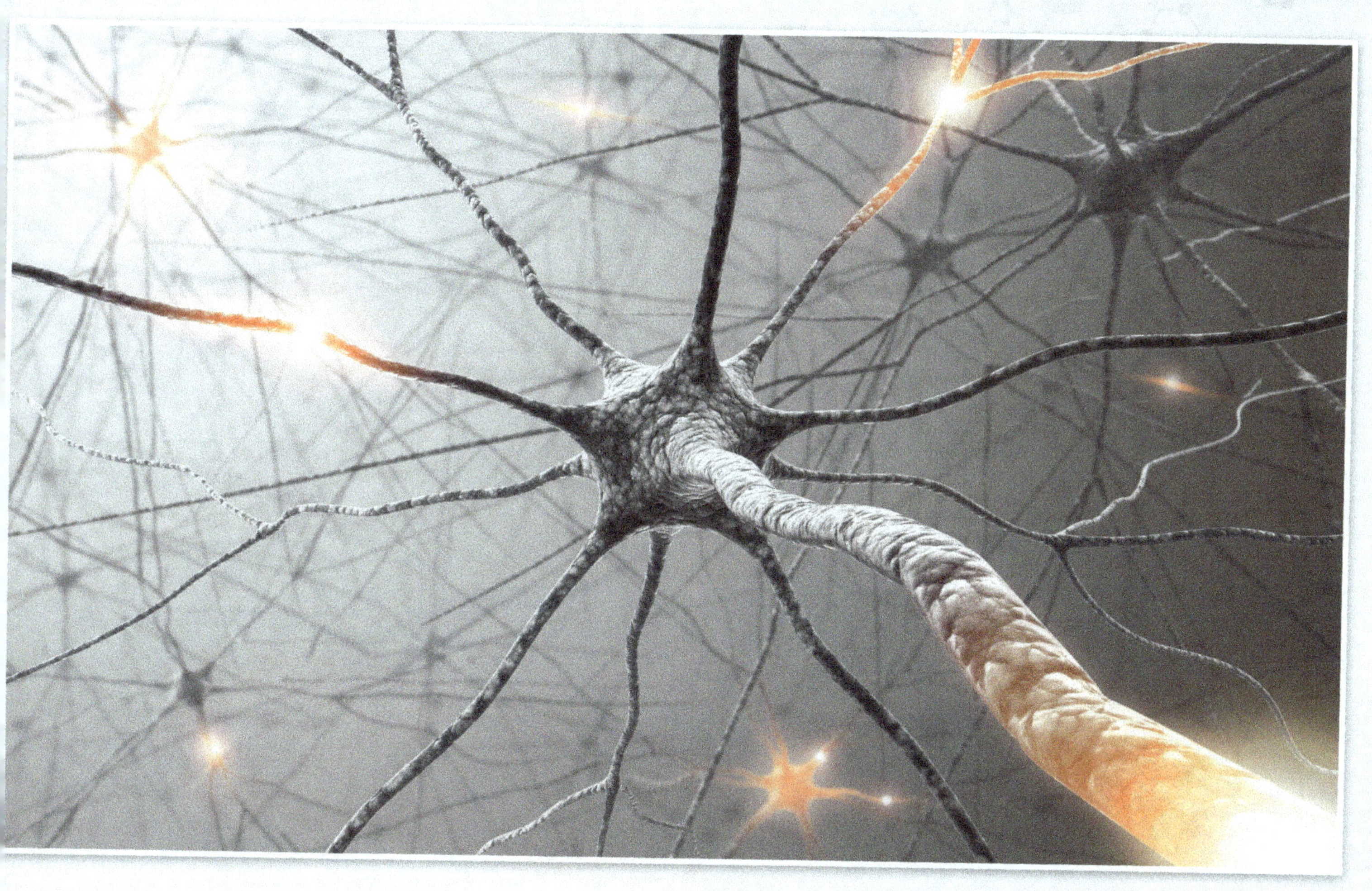

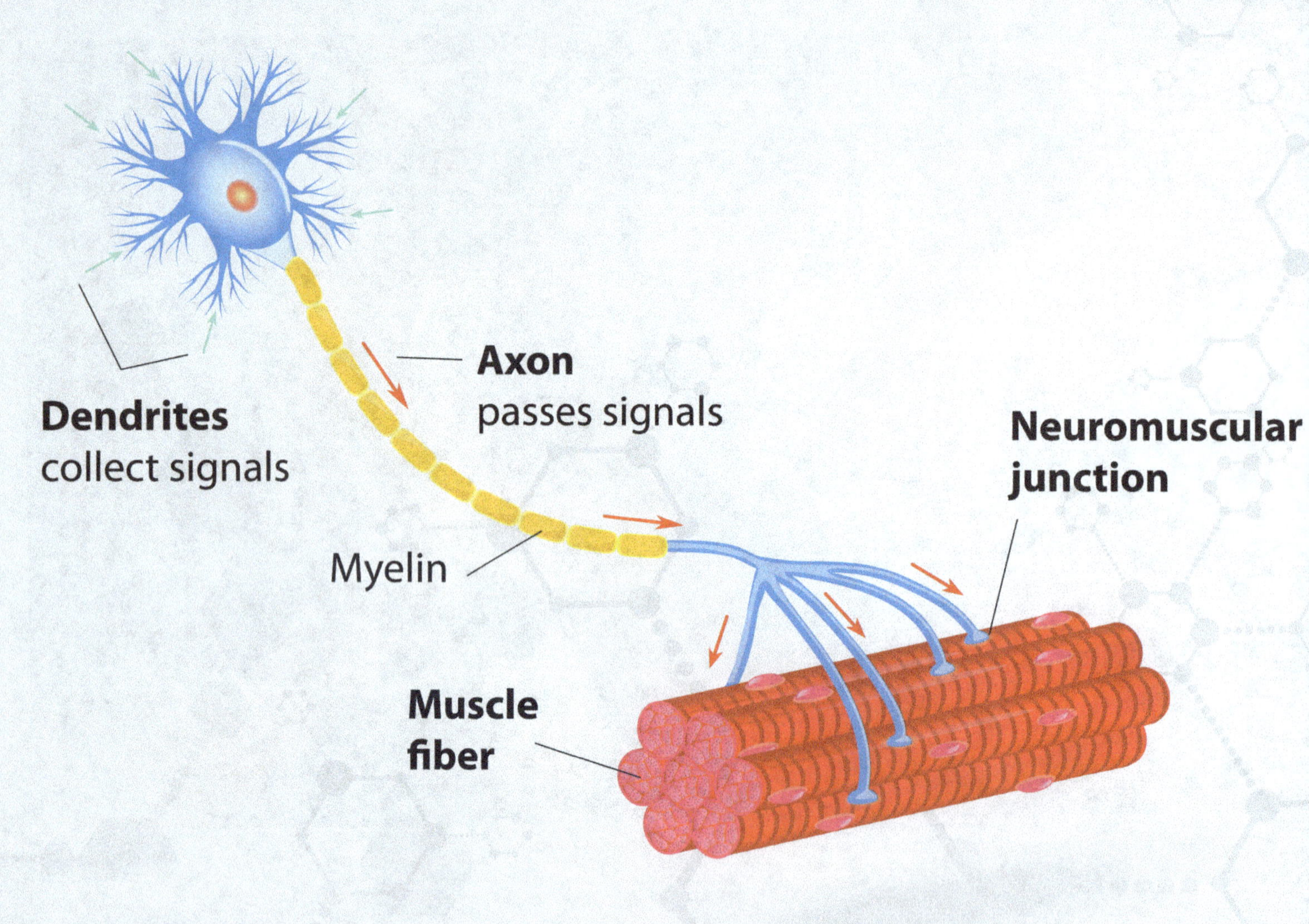

Dendrites
collect signals
Axon
passes signals
Myelin
Muscle
fiber
Neuromuscular
junction

The two key types of nerves are the sensory nerves and the motor nerves.

- **MOTOR NERVES** – Motor nerves provide for our brain to be able to control the body's muscles. The signals are sent by the brain throughout the motor nerves to indicate to our muscles to contract or expand in order for us to move.

Structure of motor neuron.

- **SENSORY NERVES** - The secondary type is referred to as the sensory nerves. They carry the impulses (signals) to our brain to indicate what is happening in the outside world. They come from our senses of ears (hear), nose (smell), tongue (taste), and skin (touch), eyes (sight).

Skin anatomy and Sensory receptors in the skin.

SENSORY RECEPTORS IN THE SKIN

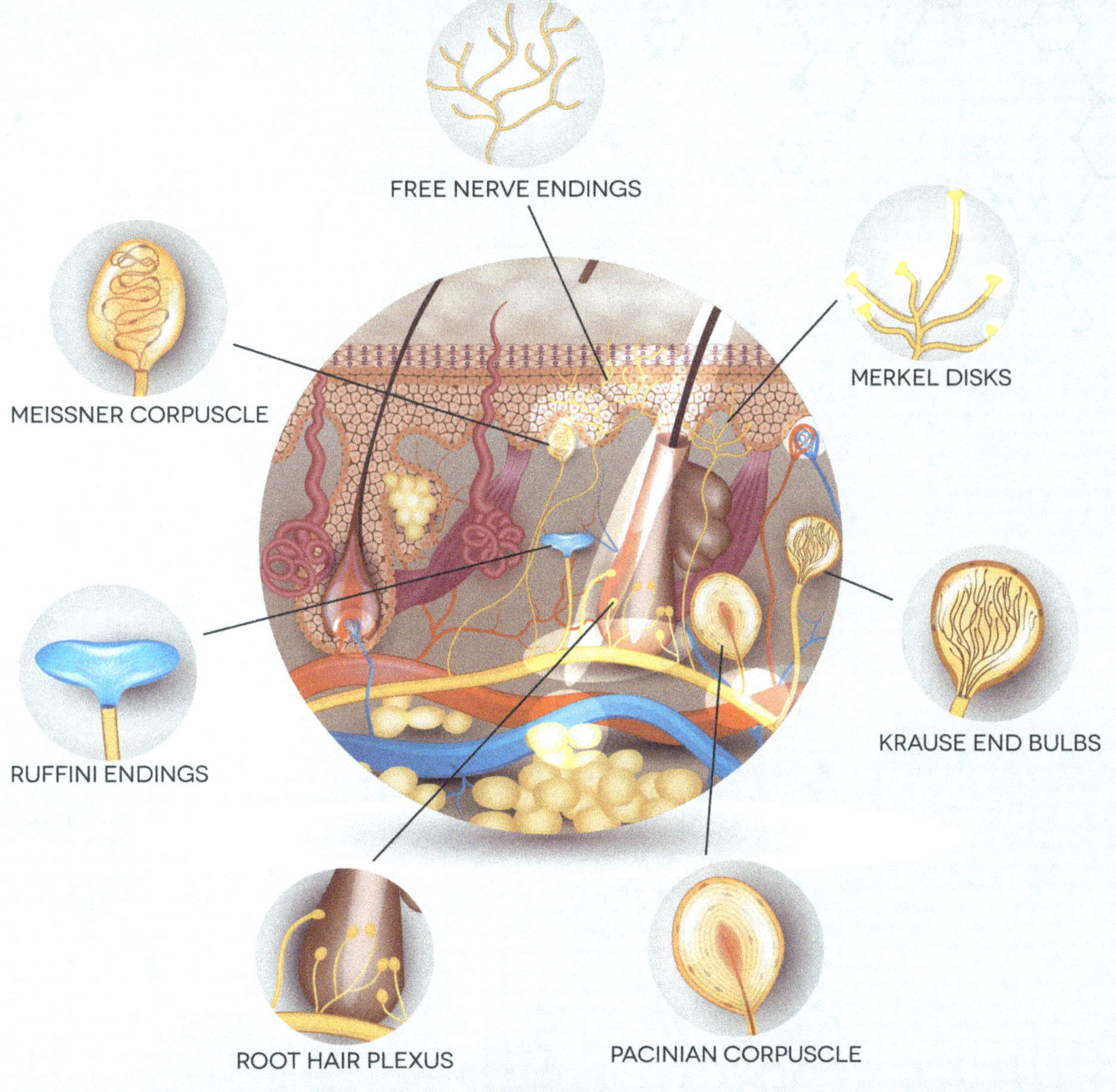

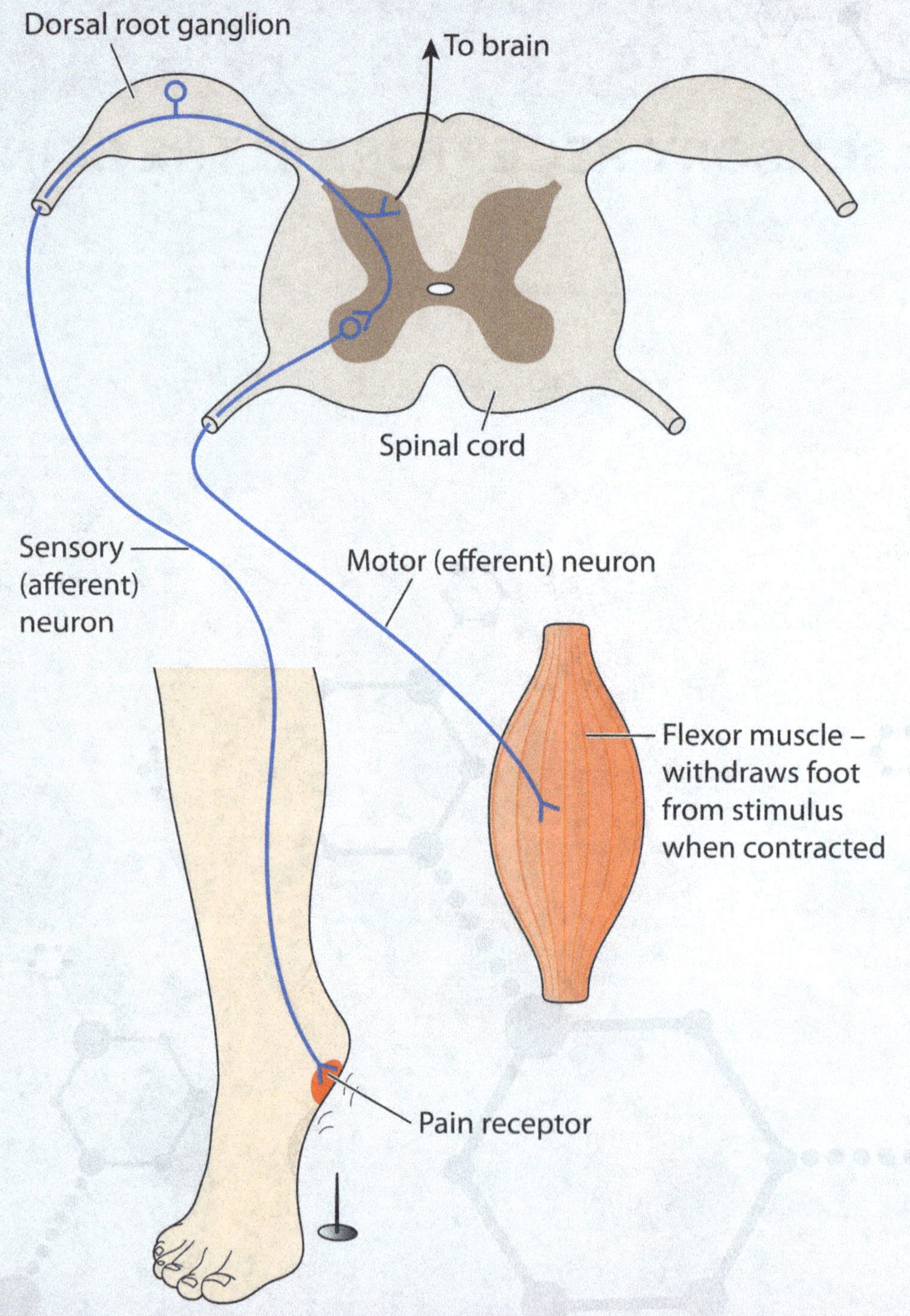

Dorsal root ganglion
To brain
Spinal cord
Sensory (afferent) neuron
Motor (efferent) neuron
Flexor muscle – withdraws foot from stimulus when contracted
Pain receptor

- **THESE SIGNALS TRAVEL IN ONLY ONE DIRECTION** - The impulses of the motor nerve travel from our brain to the muscle and the impulses of the sensory nerve travel from each of the senses to our brain.

There are two core sets of nerves residing within the peripheral nervous system – the autonomic and the somatic nervous systems.

Sensory nerve message from pain stimulus crossing spinal cord to motor neuron to effect the pain reflex.

- **AUTONOMIC NERVOUS SYSTEM** As indicated in the name, this set of nerves functions automatically, which means that we don't have to do anything, the brain does all the work. Can you imagine how much work it would take if he had to tell our heart to beat all the time or tell our digestive systems to release certain enzymes? And, what would happen if we forgot to do so? Luckily, we have the autonomic nervous system to do this for us.

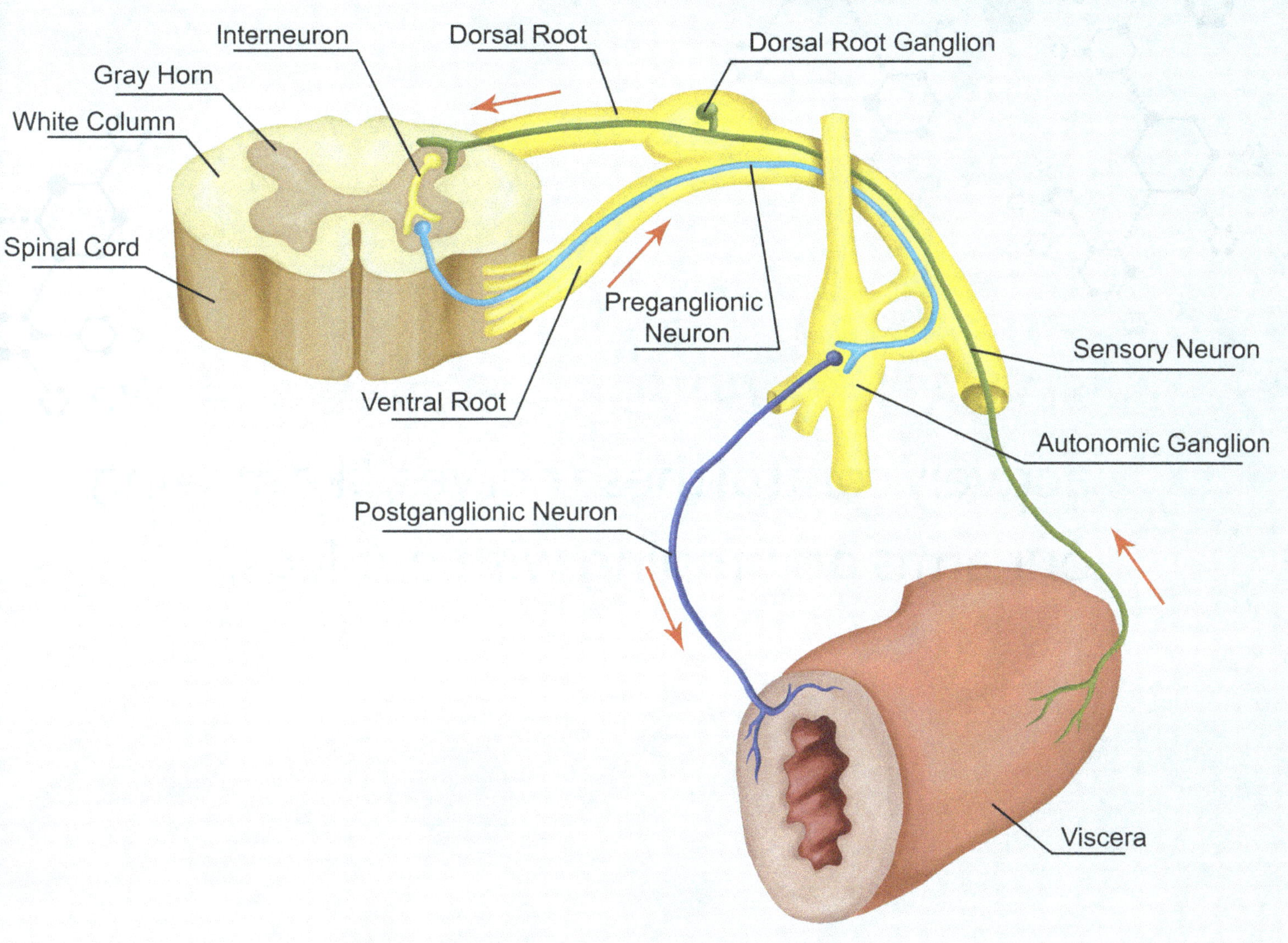

Automatic motor reflex, autonomic nervous system.

- **SOMATIC NERVOUS SYSTEM** – We actively control these nerves, like moving our arms or jumping with our legs.

Somatic motor reflex, somatic nervous system.

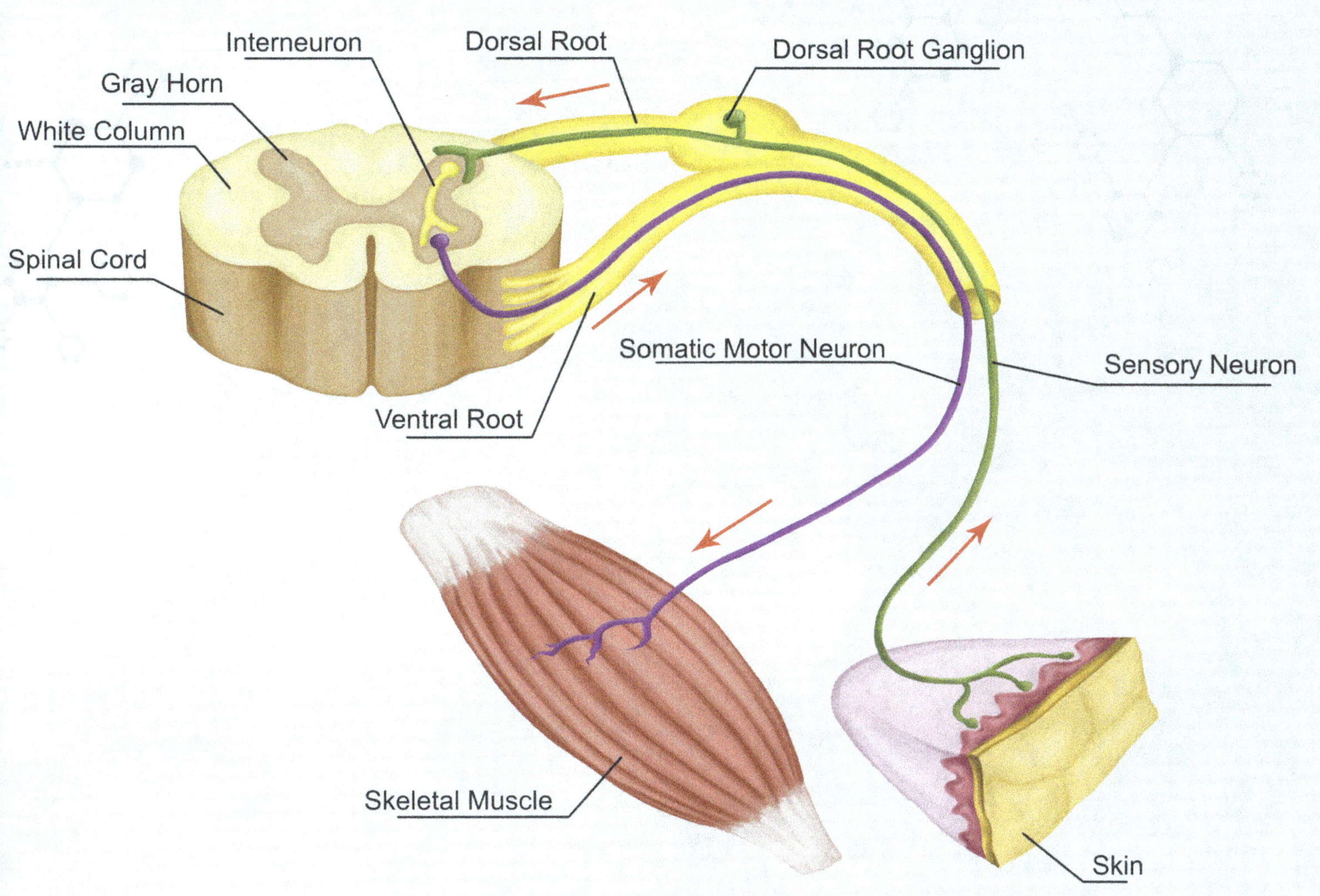

Interneuron
Gray Horn
White Column
Spinal Cord
Dorsal Root
Dorsal Root Ganglion
Somatic Motor Neuron
Sensory Neuron
Ventral Root
Skeletal Muscle
Skin

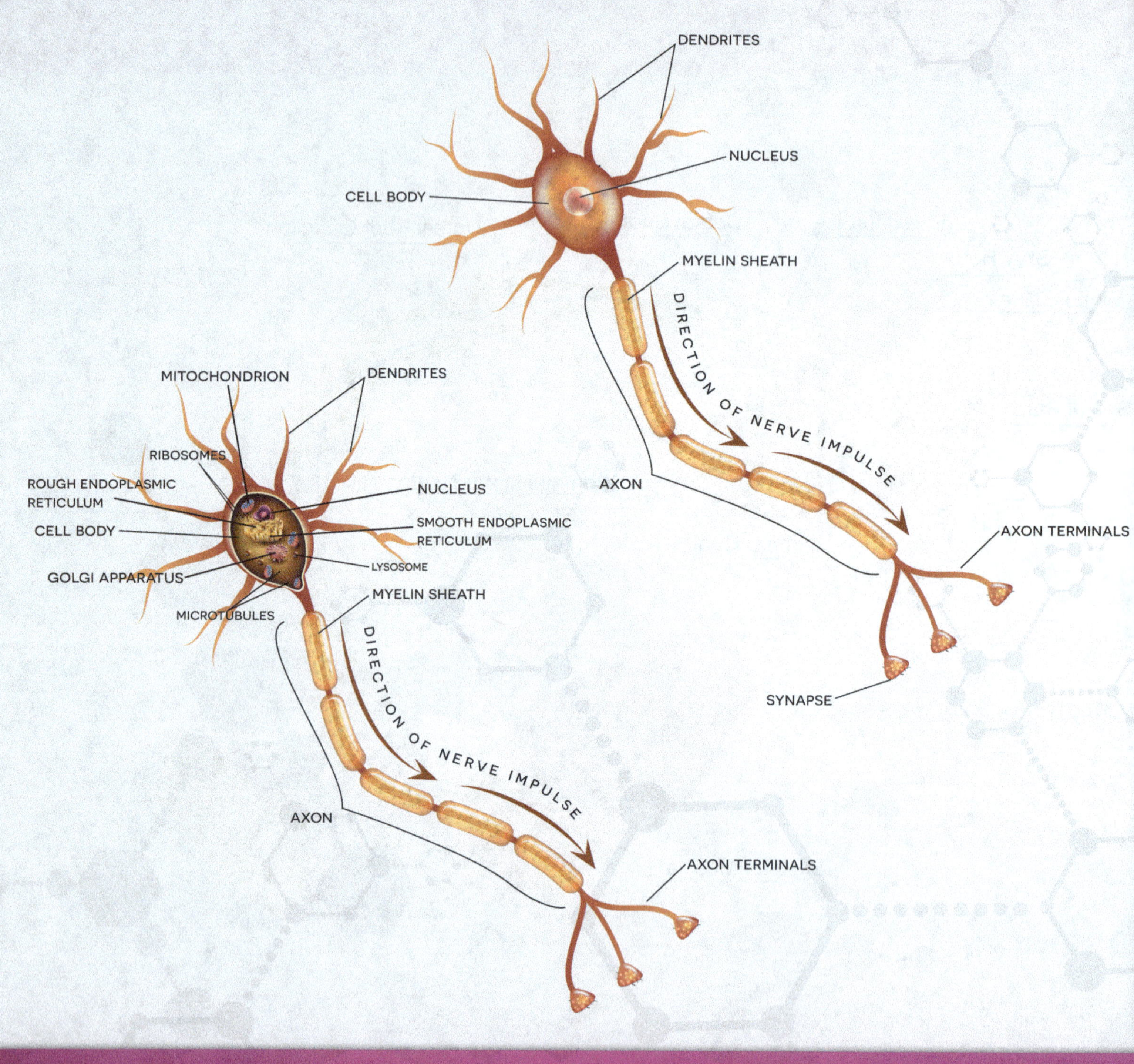
DENDRITES
NUCLEUS
CELL BODY
MYELIN SHEATH
DIRECTION OF NERVE IMPULSE
AXON
AXON TERMINALS
SYNAPSE
MITOCHONDRION
DENDRITES
RIBOSOMES
ROUGH ENDOPLASMIC RETICULUM
NUCLEUS
CELL BODY
SMOOTH ENDOPLASMIC RETICULUM
GOLGI APPARATUS
LYSOSOME
MICROTUBULES
MYELIN SHEATH
DIRECTION OF NERVE IMPULSE
AXON
AXON TERMINALS

THE NEURON

All nerves consist of several cells known as neurons. For instance, let's take a look at the motor neuron. Each one has three major parts: the axon, the cell body, and the dendrites. The dendrites are the branches that branch off the main cell body. They, then talk to the dendrites from the cell located next to them over what is known as a synapse. The axons connect to the muscles and instruct them what to do.

Neuron, nerve cell that is the main part of the nervous system.

REFLEX

Our body and its systems are very smart. Occasionally, we have to move quickly and our brain does not have time to think and our body then simply bypasses the brain. This is what happens once we touch something that is hot. Our hand moves prior to the brain telling it to. Eventually, it realizes what is happening, but the body has already done the smart thing and moved first. The doctor tests your reflexes by striking your knee in a certain area to see if your leg will move without you telling it to.

1
receptor
touching
hot object
sensory
nerve fiber
spinal cord
interneurons
grey matter
white matter
2
response
by effector
motors
nerve fiber

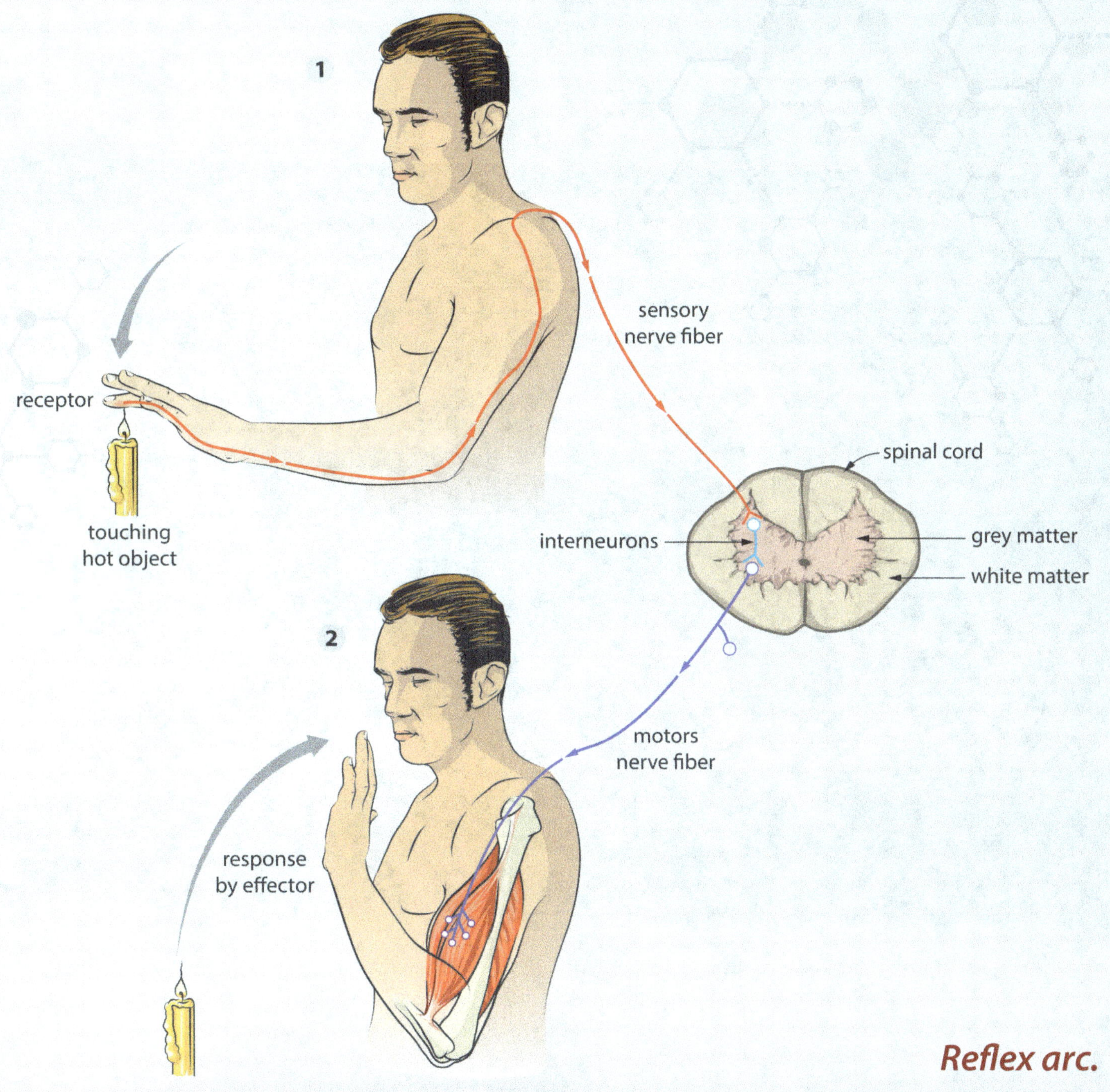

Reflex arc.

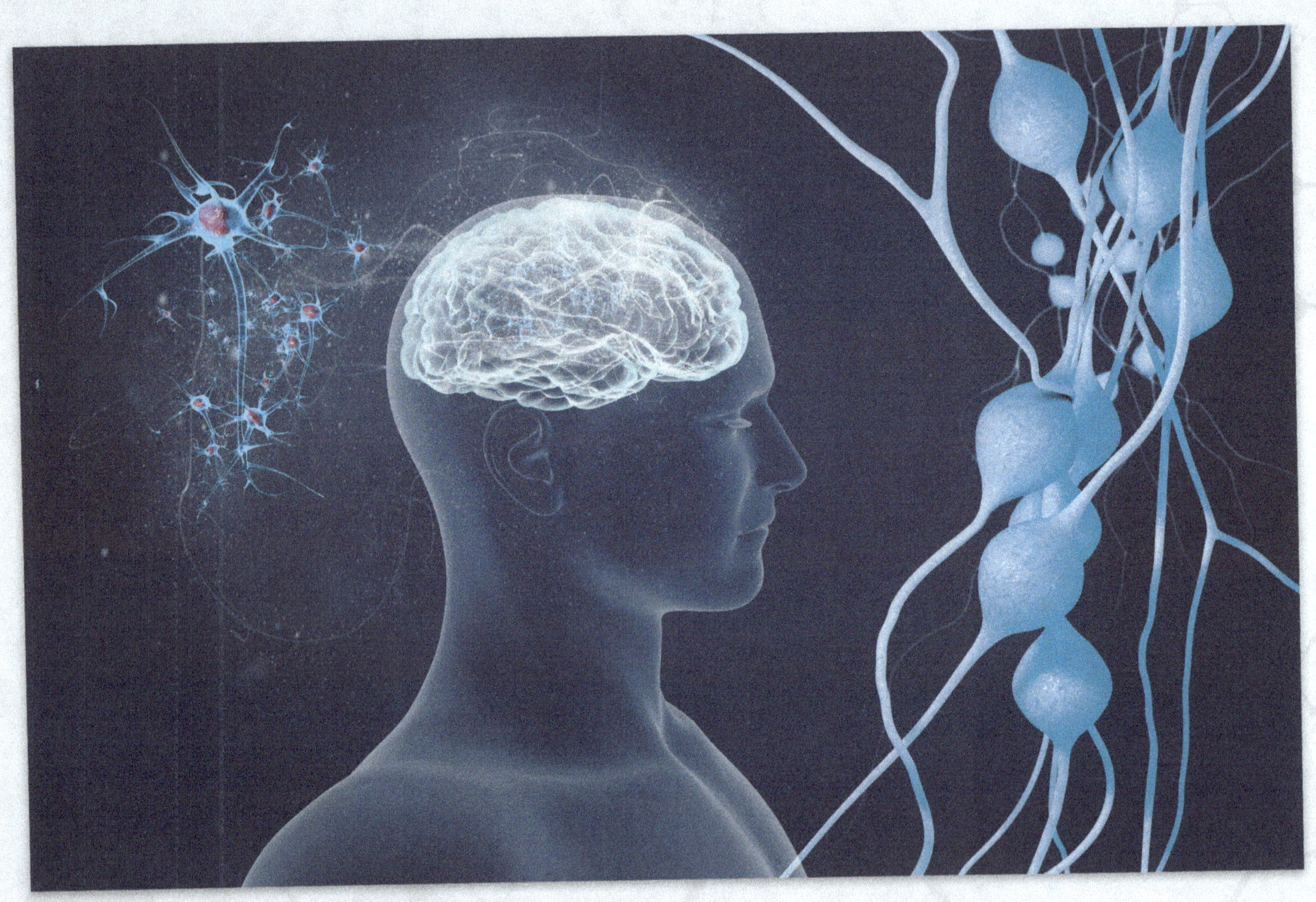

THE HUMAN BRAIN

This is where we do our thinking. Our five senses are all tied into it which allows us to be able to experience the world outside. We solve problems, have emotions, remember, dream about the future, worry about stuff, and control our bodies from our brain.

Human brain and its capabilities.

Even though it is an amazing organ, it doesn't look so great. It is a gray-looking ball of wrinkled tissue and it is approximately the size of two fists that are put together. It sits in our thick, hard skull, with fluid and membranes surrounding it for protection.

Noxious and pain receptors in skin and the nerve pathways to the brain, via the spinal cord and thalamus.

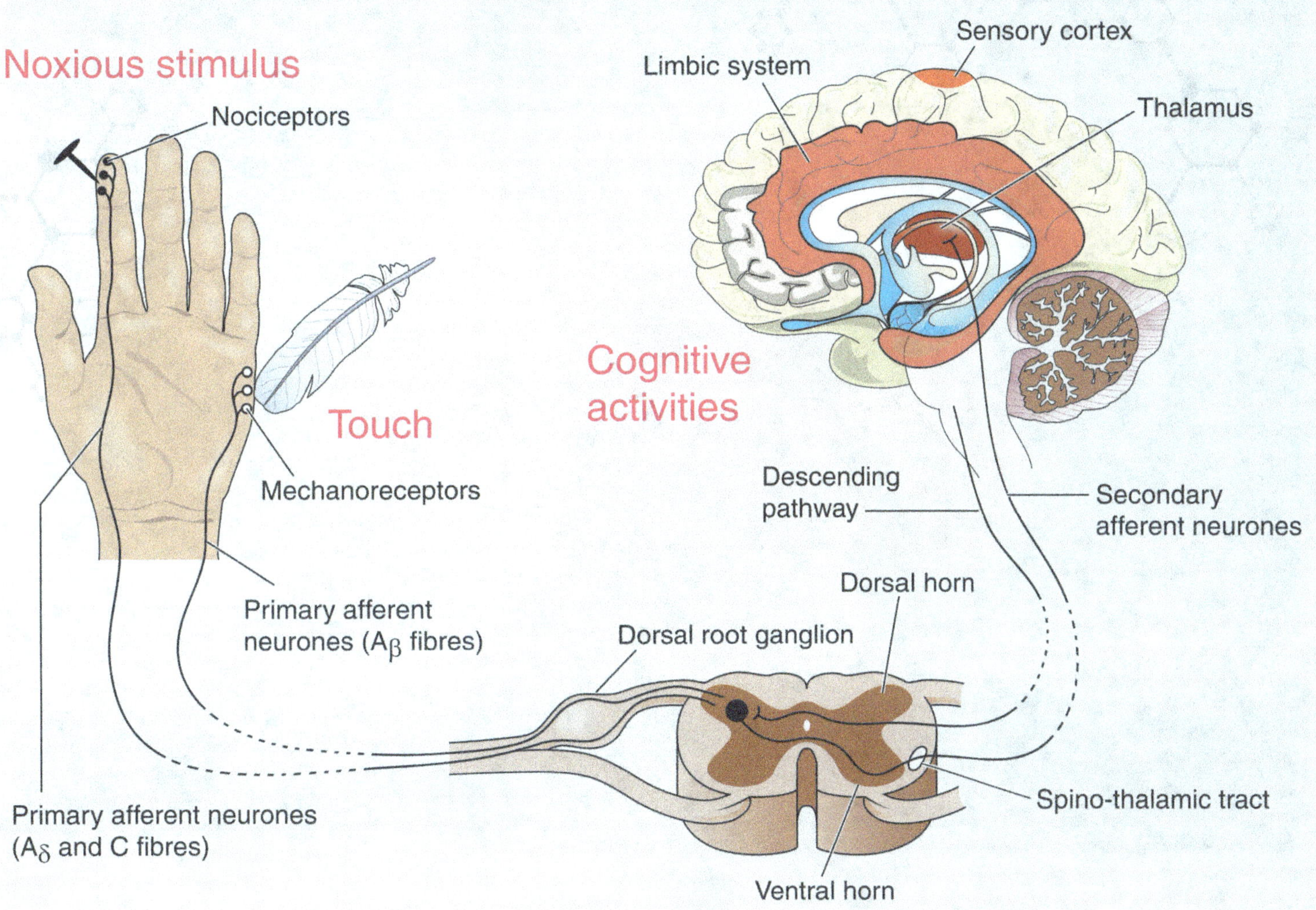

Noxious stimulus
Nociceptors
Touch
Mechanoreceptors
Primary afferent
neurones (A$_\beta$ fibres)
Primary afferent neurones
(A$_\delta$ and C fibres)
Limbic system
Sensory cortex
Thalamus
Cognitive
activities
Descending
pathway
Secondary
afferent neurones
Dorsal horn
Dorsal root ganglion
Spino-thalamic tract
Ventral horn

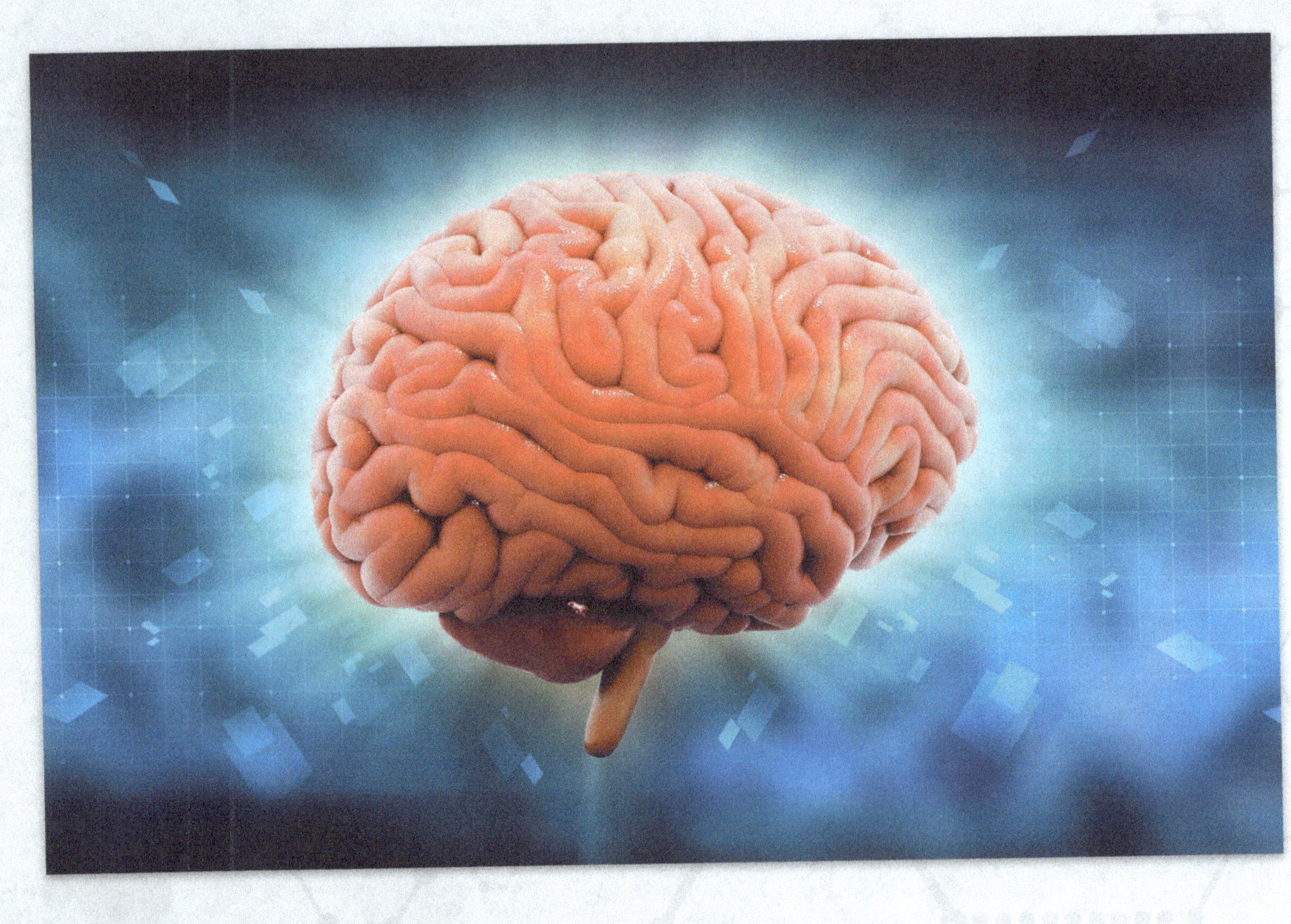

HOW DOES THE BRAIN COMMUNICATE?

As we discussed earlier, it is part of our nervous system. Along with the spinal cord, they make up our central nervous system. Our brain connects with nerves that travel around our body. Nerves from the senses (touch, hearing, seeing, etc.) send impulses to our brain and let it know what's going on in the world around us. It also transmits impulses to muscles by using nerves, to make our body move.

Digital illustration of brain in color background.

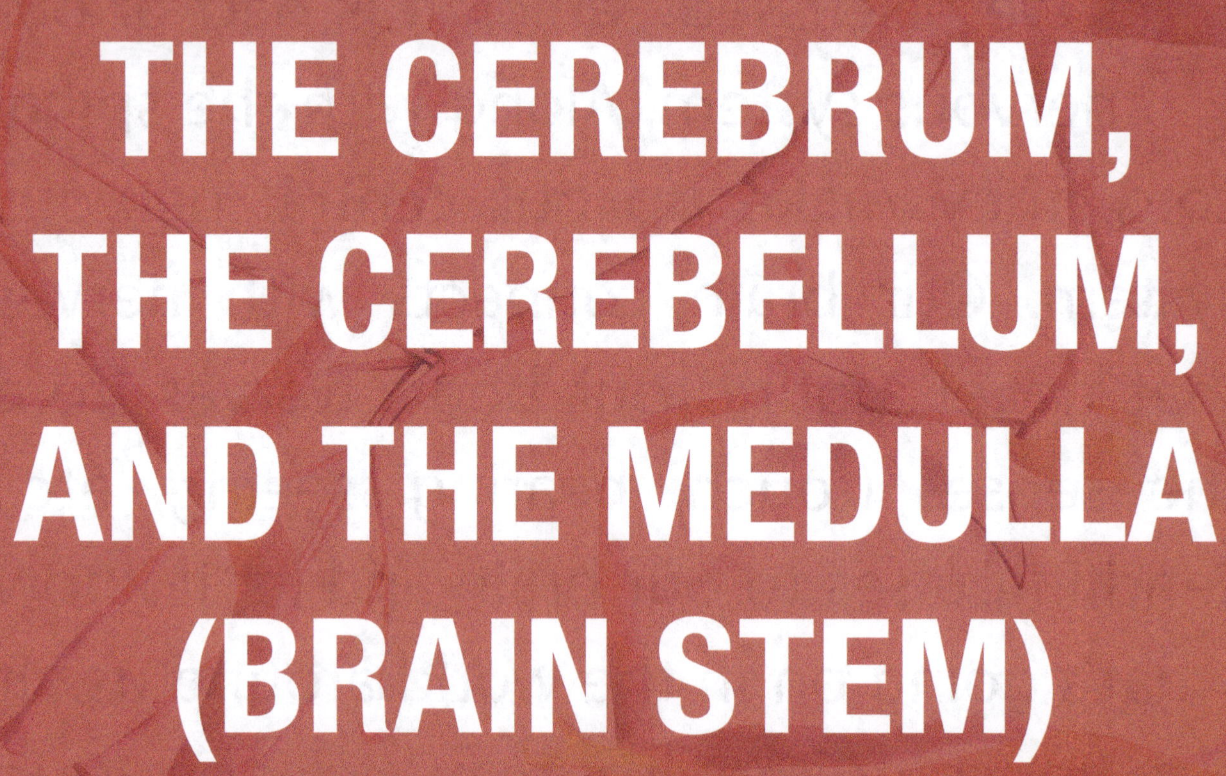

Pulses of neurons in the brain.

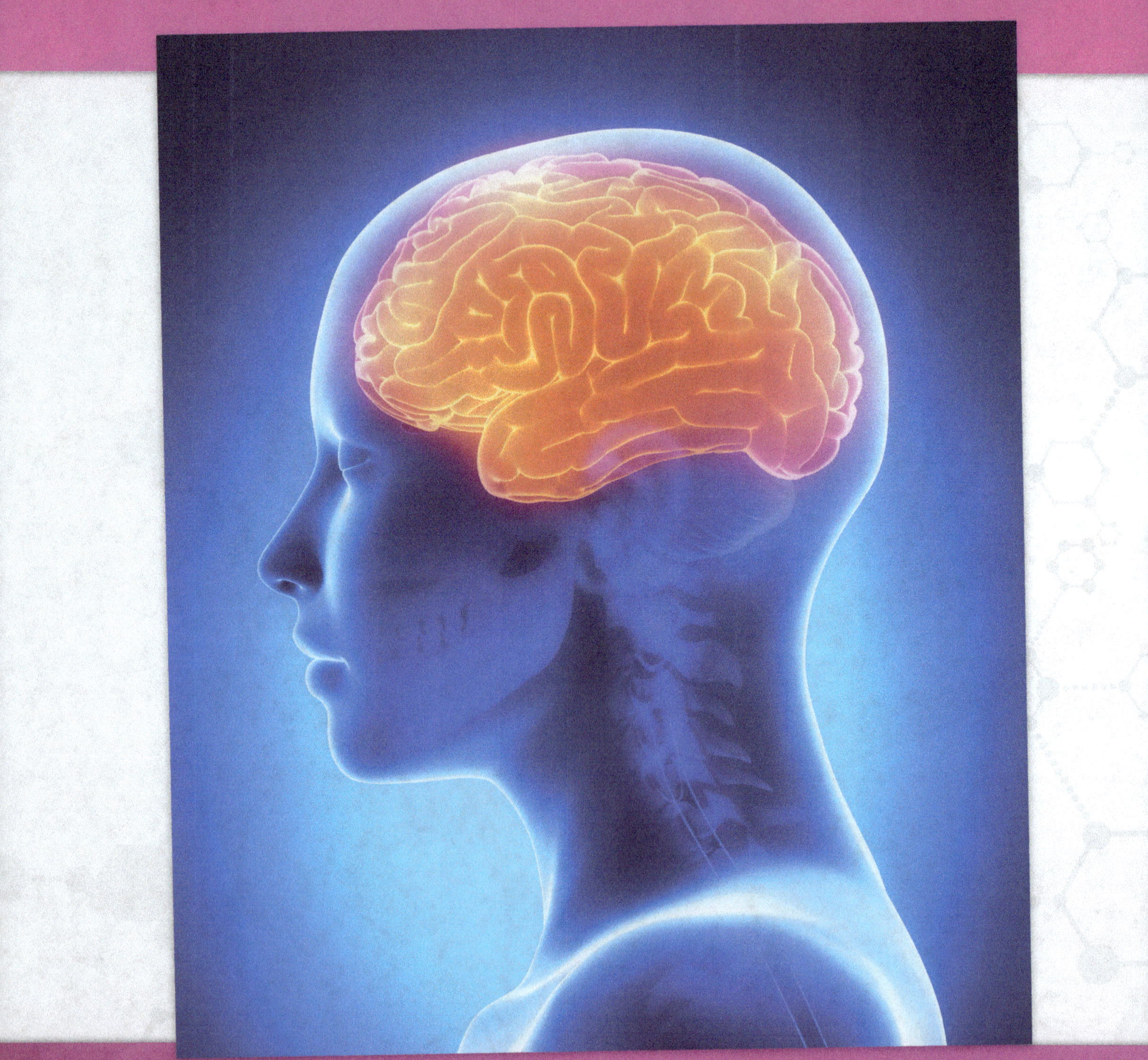

- **CEREBRUM** - This is the largest part of our brain and is also the wrinkly gray part. Different sections of it deal with different sections of our body. The back part works with our vision, while other parts work with functions like hearing, movement, touch, and language. Intelligent or smart people are often referred to as being cerebral.

Cerebrum - brain anatomy.

- **CEREBELLUM** - The cerebellum is located at the bottom and back of the brain and works with motor movement. It takes care of incoming motor messages from our nerves and decides what has to be done. It can learn motor skills with practice which allows us to do things like typing or riding a bike, without thinking about it.

Cerebellum - brain anatomy.

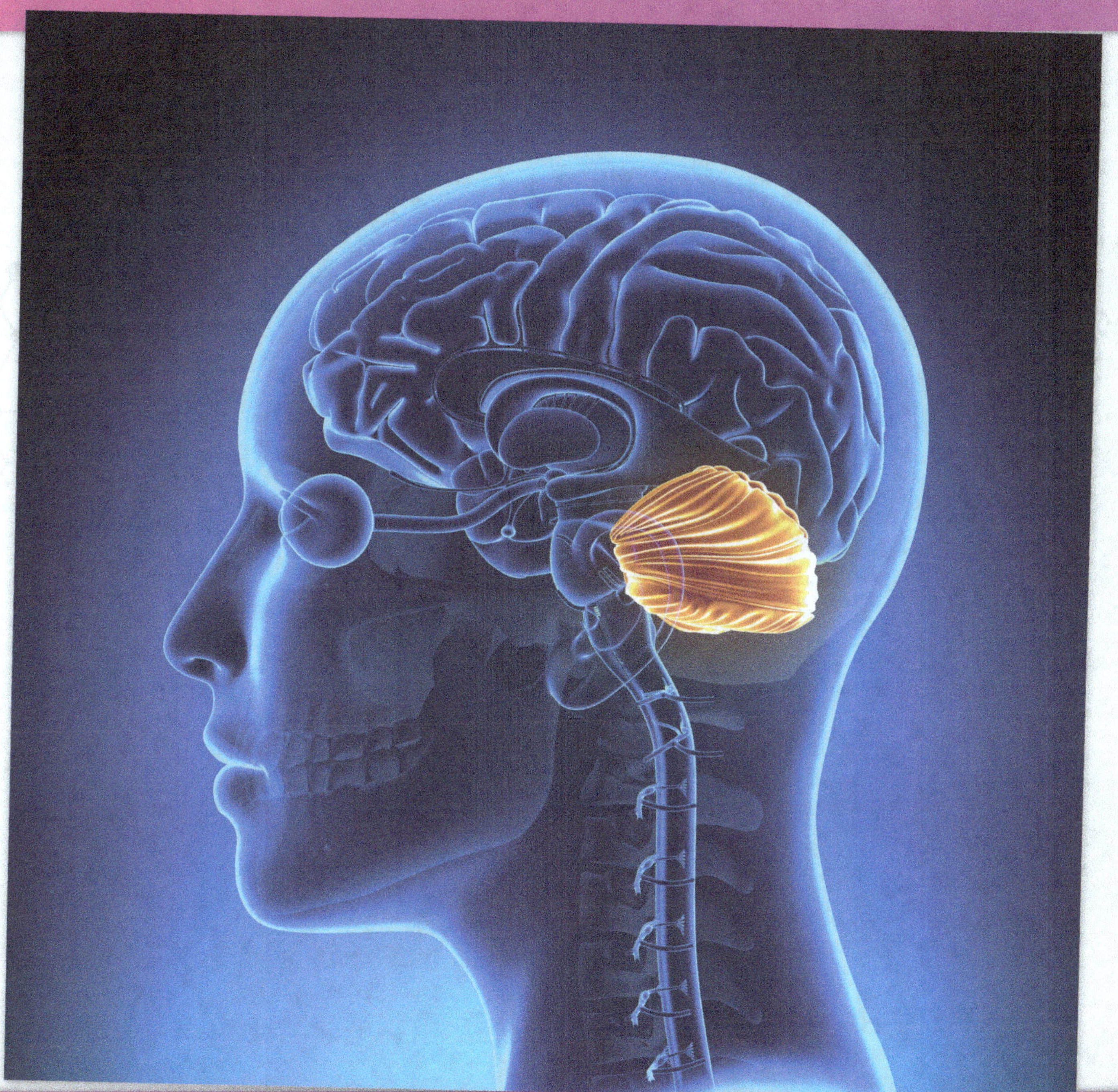

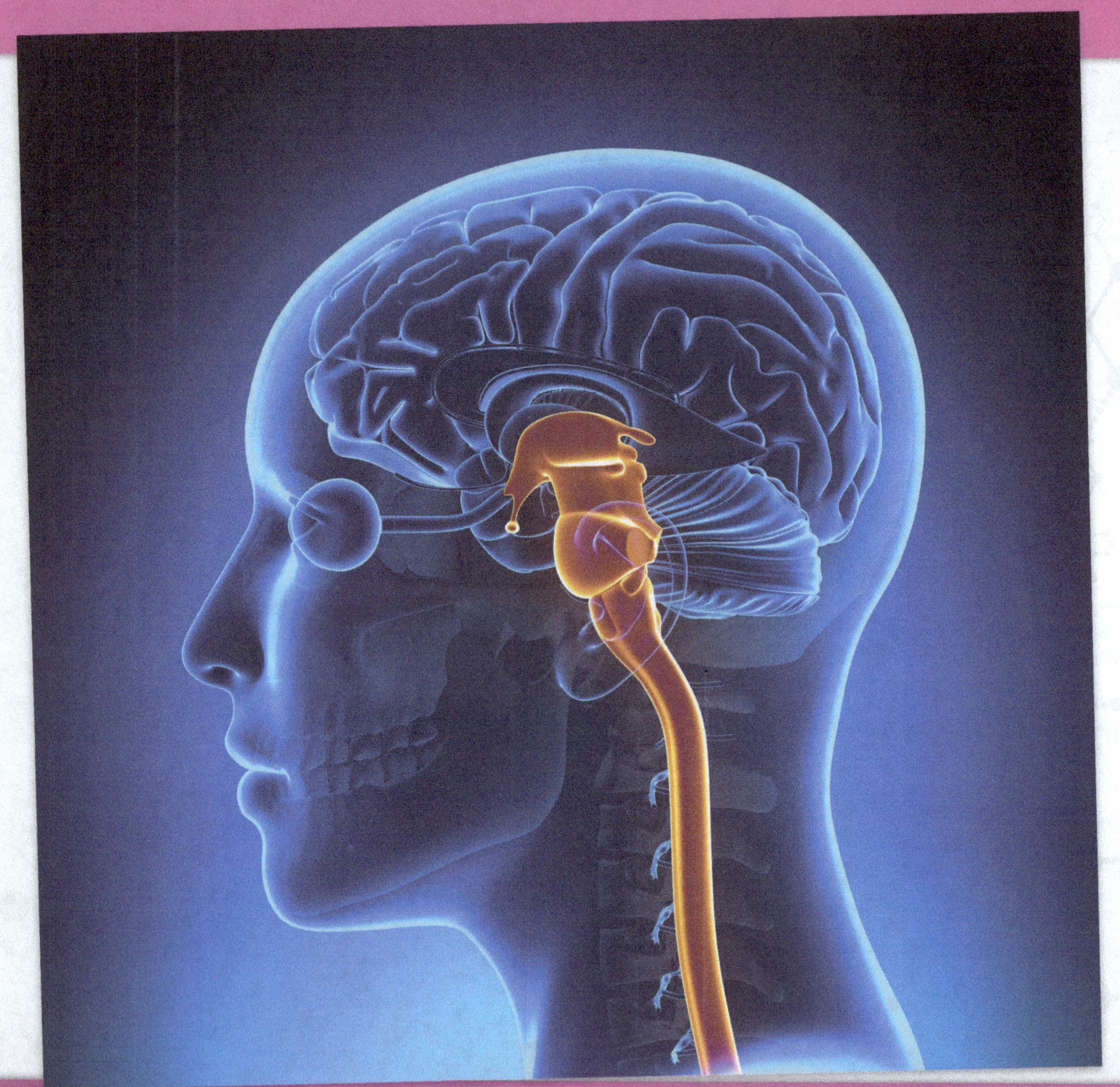

- ## BRAIN STEM OR MEDULLA

This is the location where the brain is connected to our spinal cord. Additionally, many functions which are automatic are controlled here such as breathing, digesting food, and making sure the heart is beating.

Brain Stem - brain anatomy.

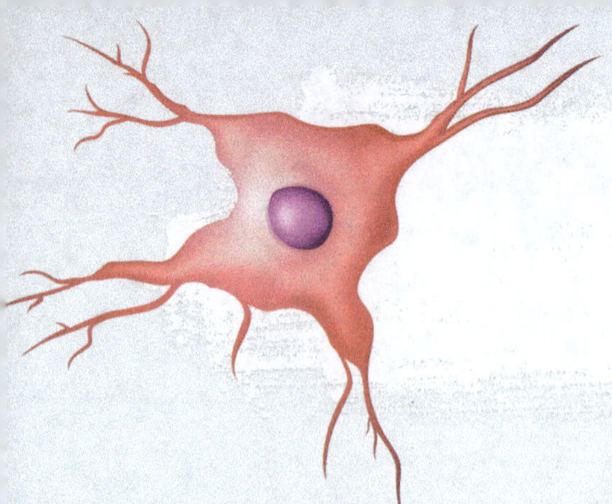

MEMORY

Our brain has two different types of memory; long term and short term. While scientists are still researching exactly how it works, they do know that our short-term memory provides us with the ability to remember things for a very short time without practicing or rehearsing it.

Conceptual image of a man from side profile showing brain and brain activity.

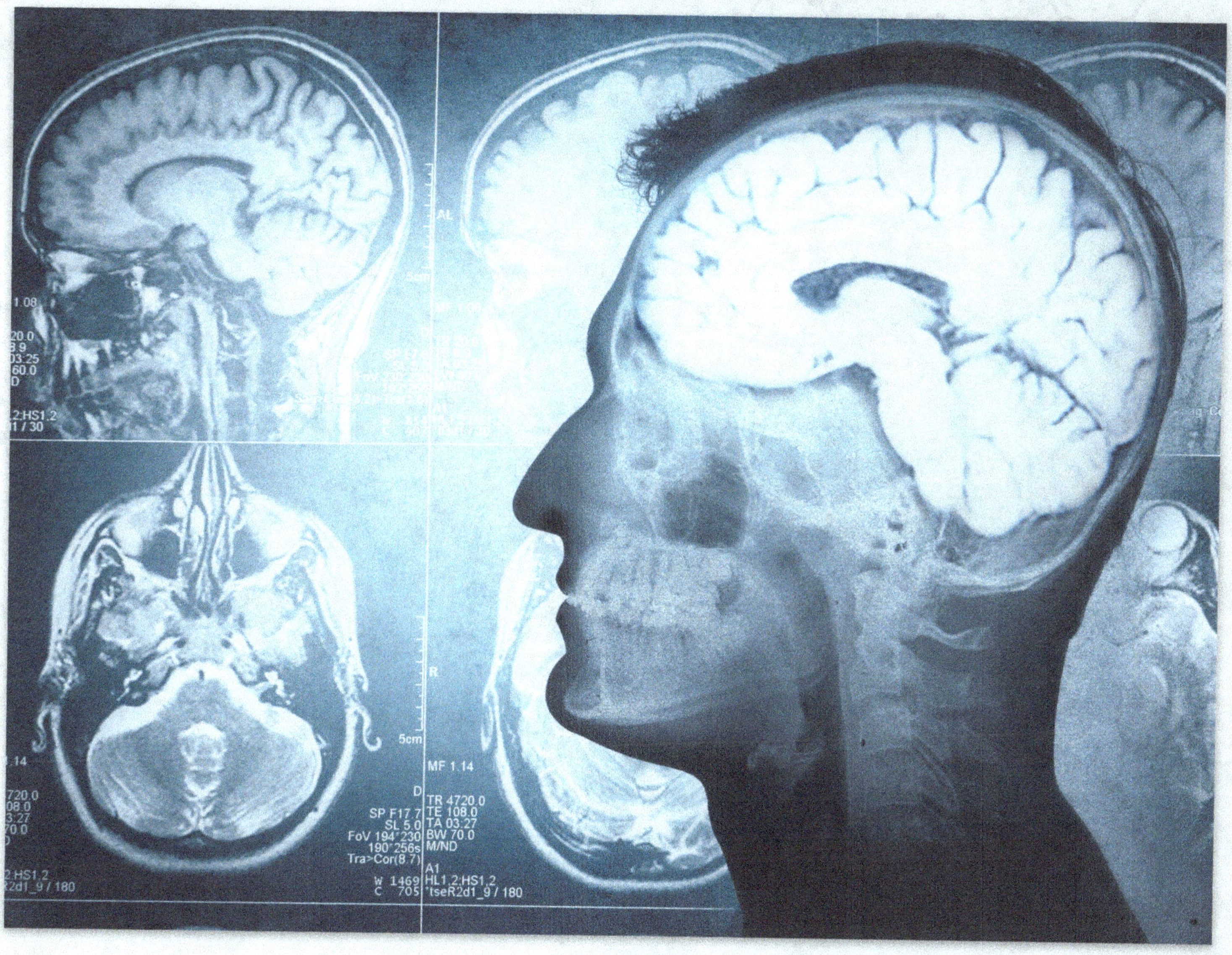

1.08
20.0
8.9
03:25
60.0
D
.2:HS1.2
1 / 30
AL
5cm
SE
R
D
.14
720.0
08.0
3:27
70.0
D
2:HS1.2
2d1_9 / 180
MF 1.14
SP F17.7
SL 5.0
FoV 194*230
190*256s
Tra>Cor(8.7)
A1
W 1469
C 705
TR 4720.0
TE 108.0
TA 03:27
BW 70.0
M/ND
A1
HL1.2:HS1.2
*tseR2d1_9 / 180

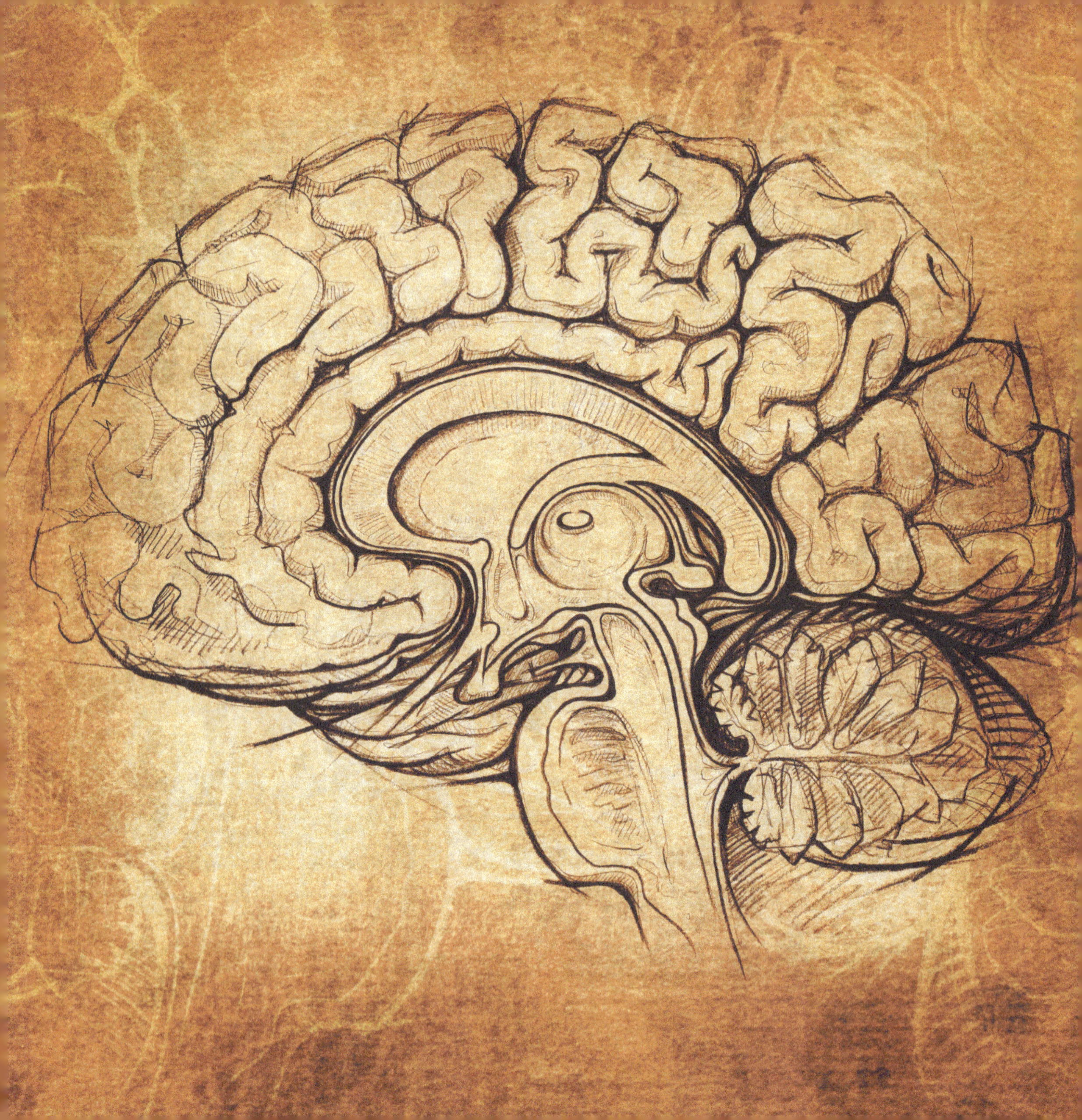

THE NEED FOR ENERGY

While it may not move, our brain requires a lot of energy. The blood sends the energy to our brain using the blood vessels and this occurs all the time. Our brain uses approximately 20% of the energy of our body.

Human brain sagittal view medical sketch.

HUMAN BODY

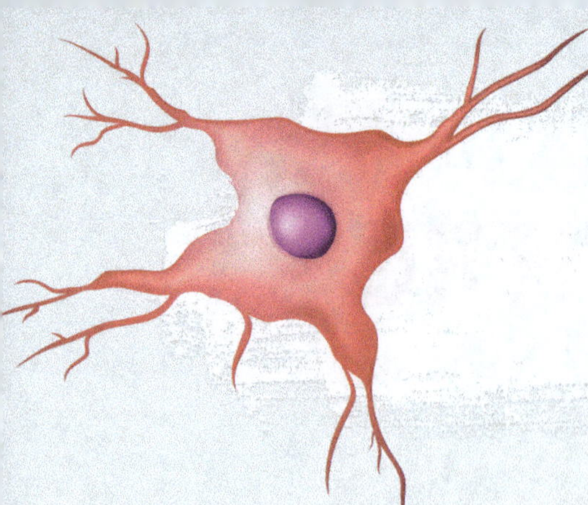

Our human body consists of a complex biological system that involves organs, tissues, cells, and systems that all work together to create a human being.

Neurons - Synapse in human neural system.

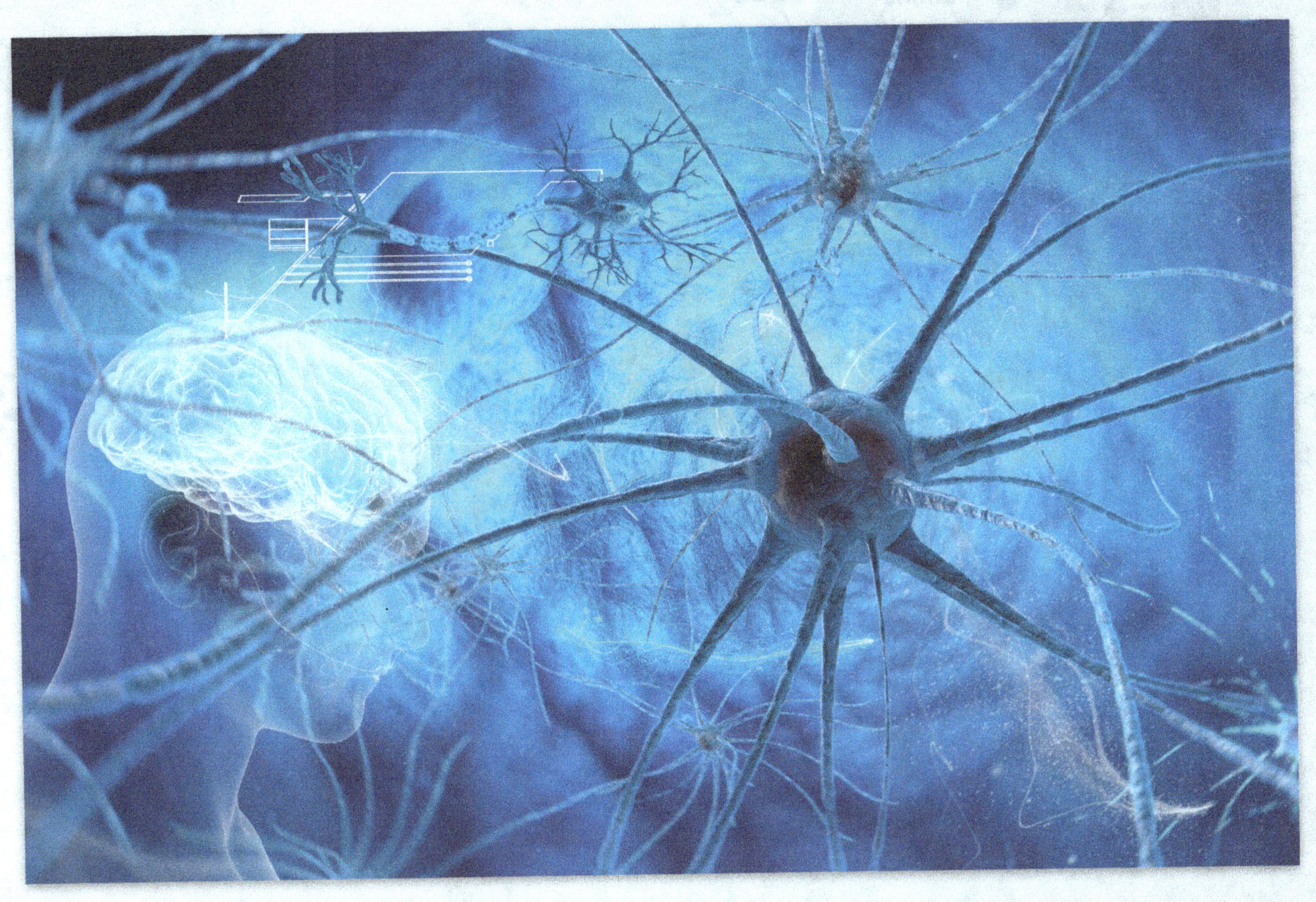

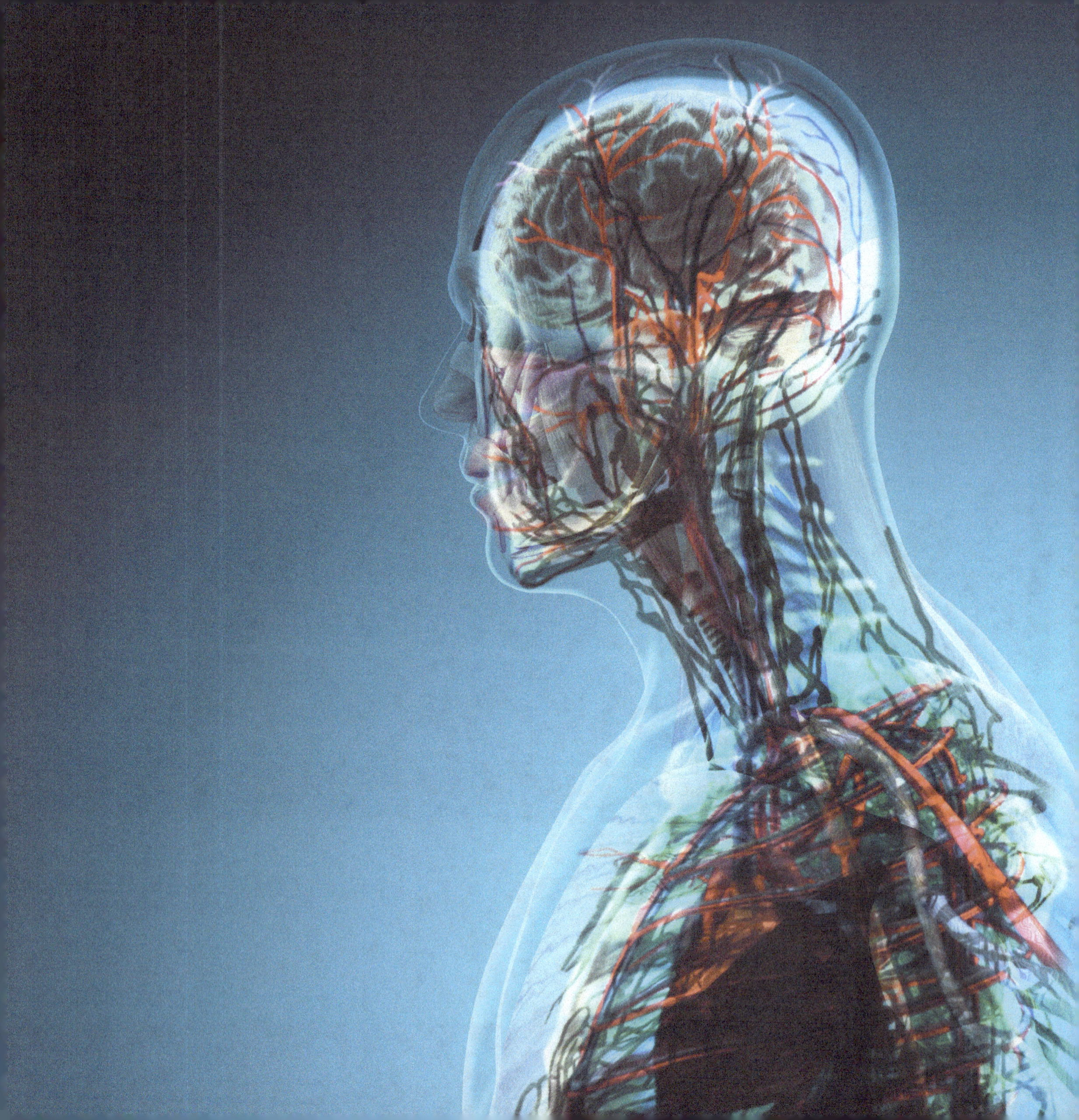

THE MAIN STRUCTURES OF THE HUMAN BODY

Our body can be separated into many key structures from the outside. The brain, which controls our body, is housed in our head. The trunk and neck house several important systems that keeps our body healthy and alive. The arms and legs (limbs) help our bodies to move about function in the outside world.

The human body (organs) by X-ray.

THE FIVE SENSES

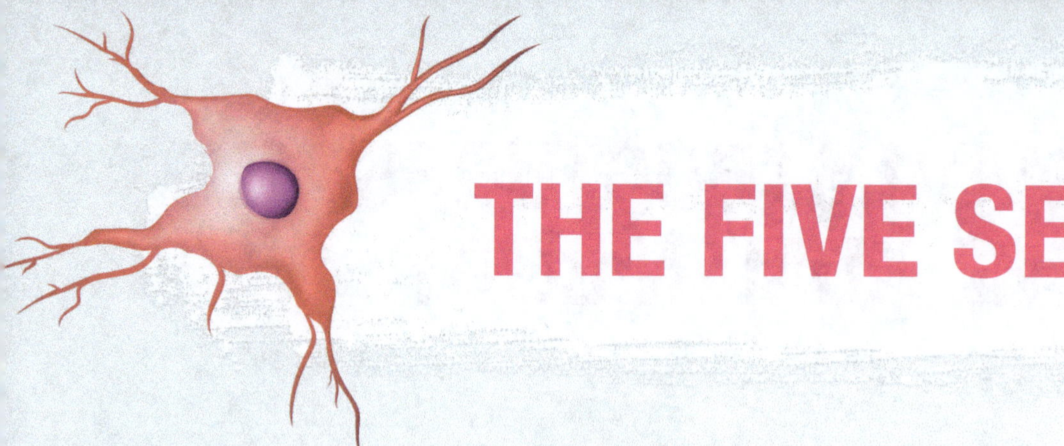

We have five main senses that are used to convey information from the outside world to our brain. These five senses include *hearing (ears), sight (eyes), smell (nose), touch (skin),* and *taste (tongue).*

Five senses line icons.

FIVE SENSES LINE ICONS

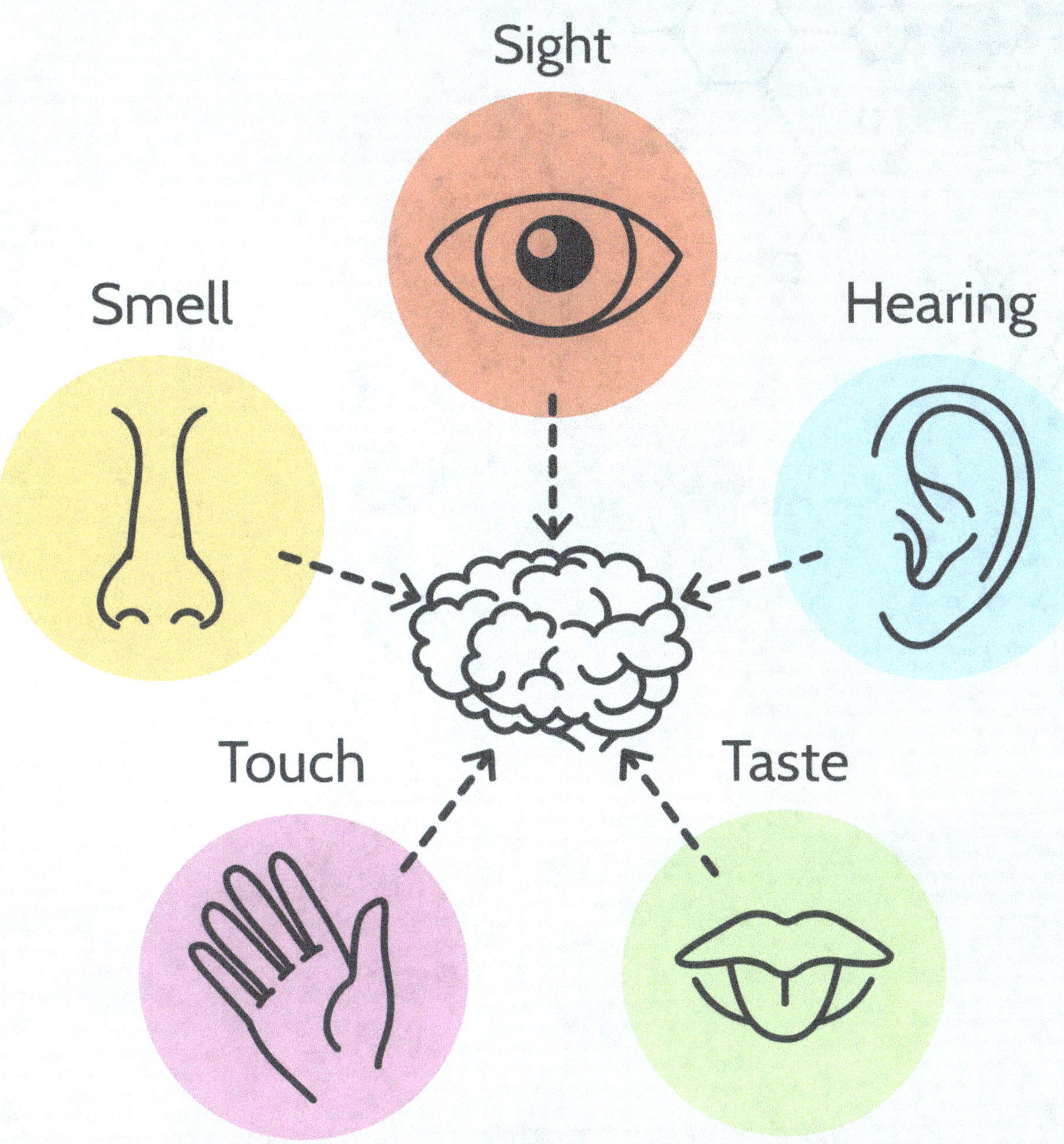

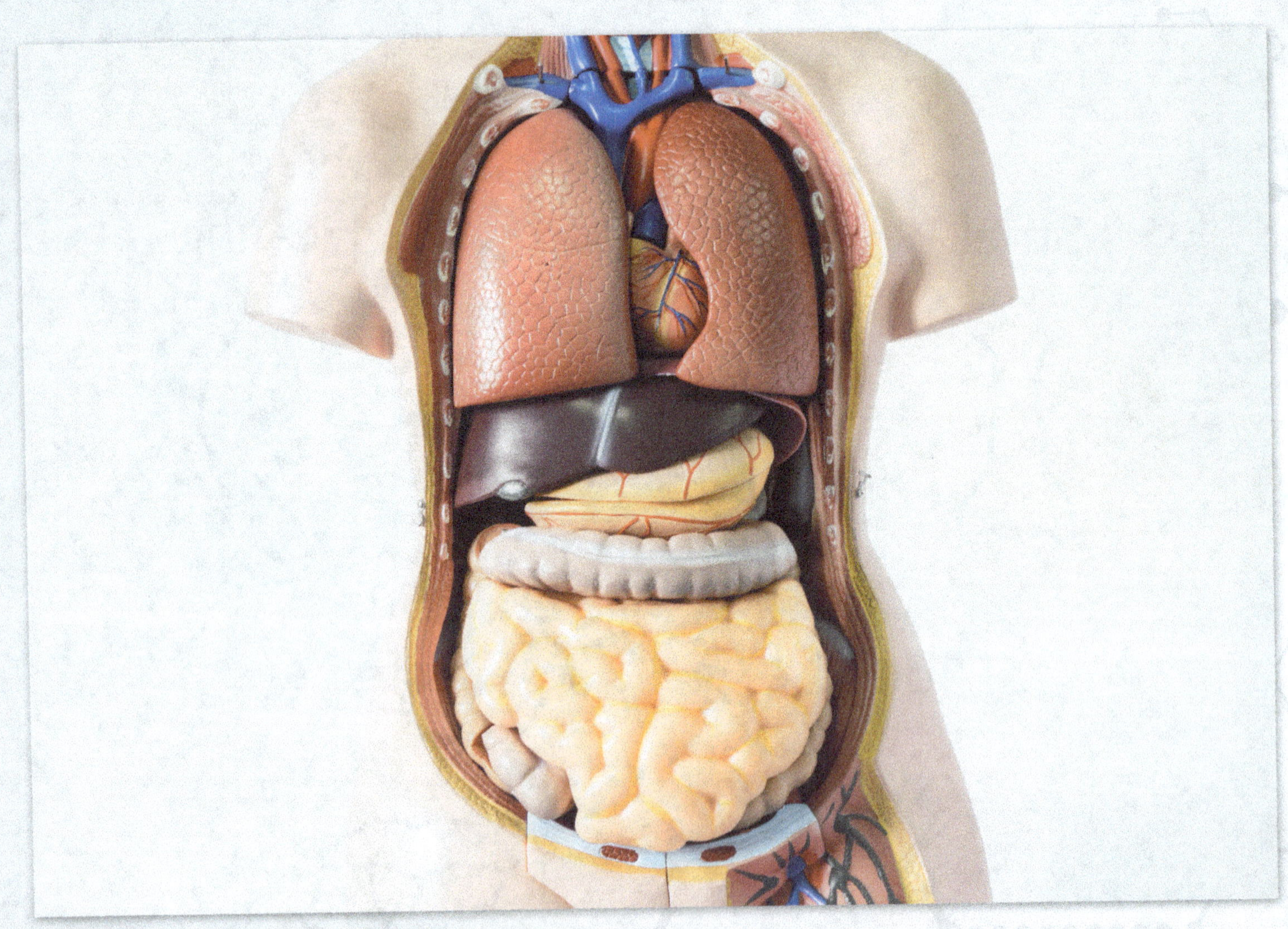

Anatomy of a human body model.

ORGAN SYSTEMS

Our body is made up of many organ systems. Each one consists of organs and other structures in the body that work together in order to perform a function. Scientists mostly divide it into 11 different systems.

The skeletal system consists of tendons, ligaments, and bones and supports the body's overall structure and protects its organs.

The muscular system works closely in conjunction with the skeletal system and helps the body with movement and its ability to interact with the outside world.

The Circulatory (Cardiovascular) system helps to deliver the nutrients throughout our body and consists of the blood vessels, blood, and heart.

Cartoon illustration of human circulatory system for kids.

Circulatory system

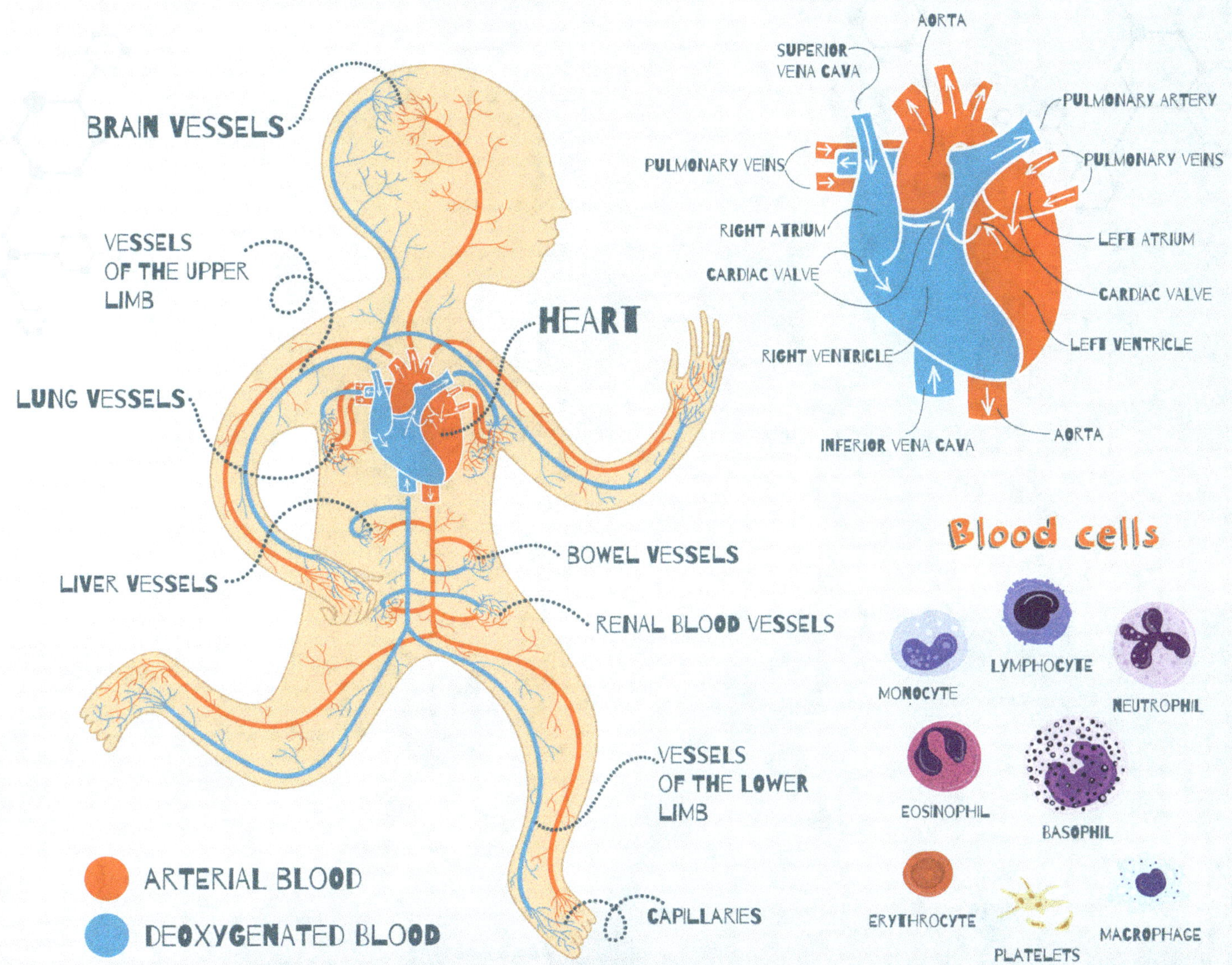

Nervous system

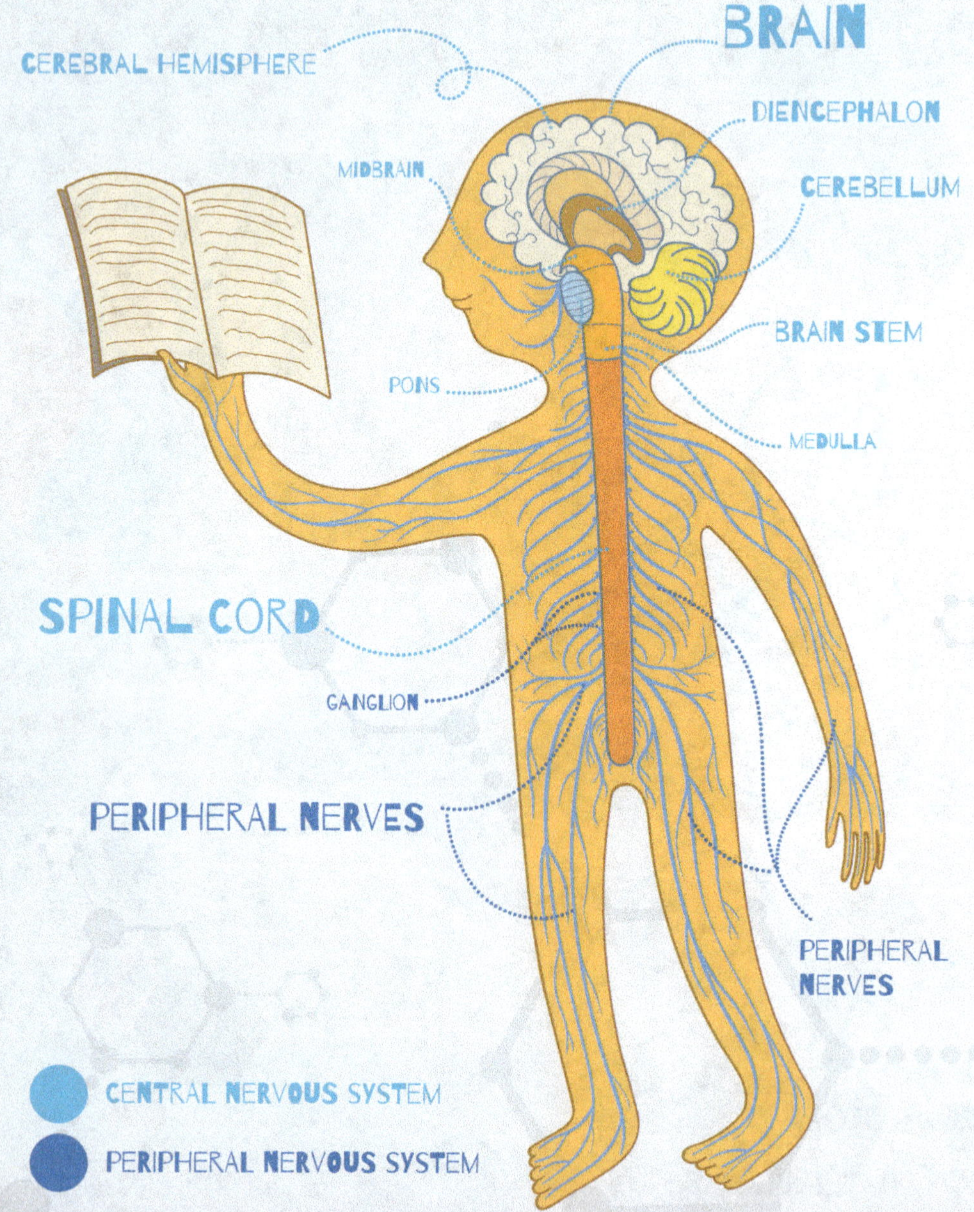

The digestive system works in converting food into energy and nutrients that our bodies need. The stomach, pancreas, liver, large intestine, and small intestine are of some of the organs of our digestive system.

The nervous system works with our body to communicate as well as allowing the brain to control the many functions of the human body. Included in this system are the spinal cord, the brain, and a large network of nerves.

Cartoon illustration of human nervous system for kids.

The respiratory system brings the oxygen into our body via the lungs and windpipe and then removes any carbon dioxide from our body.

The endocrine system is the system that produces hormones needed to regulate other systems in our body, and includes the pituitary gland, thyroid, adrenal glands, pancreas, to name a few.

Cartoon illustration of endocrine system.

Endocrine system

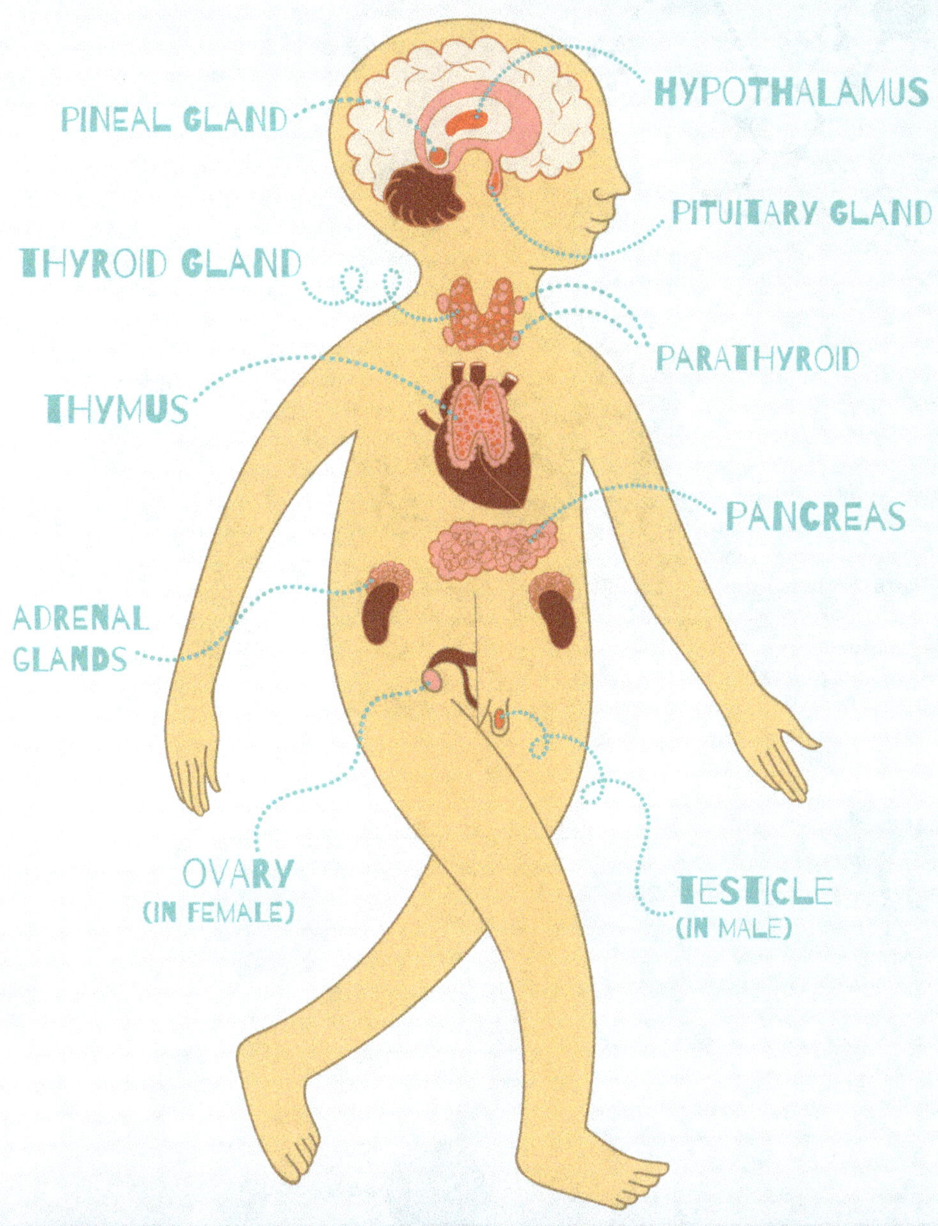

Digestive system

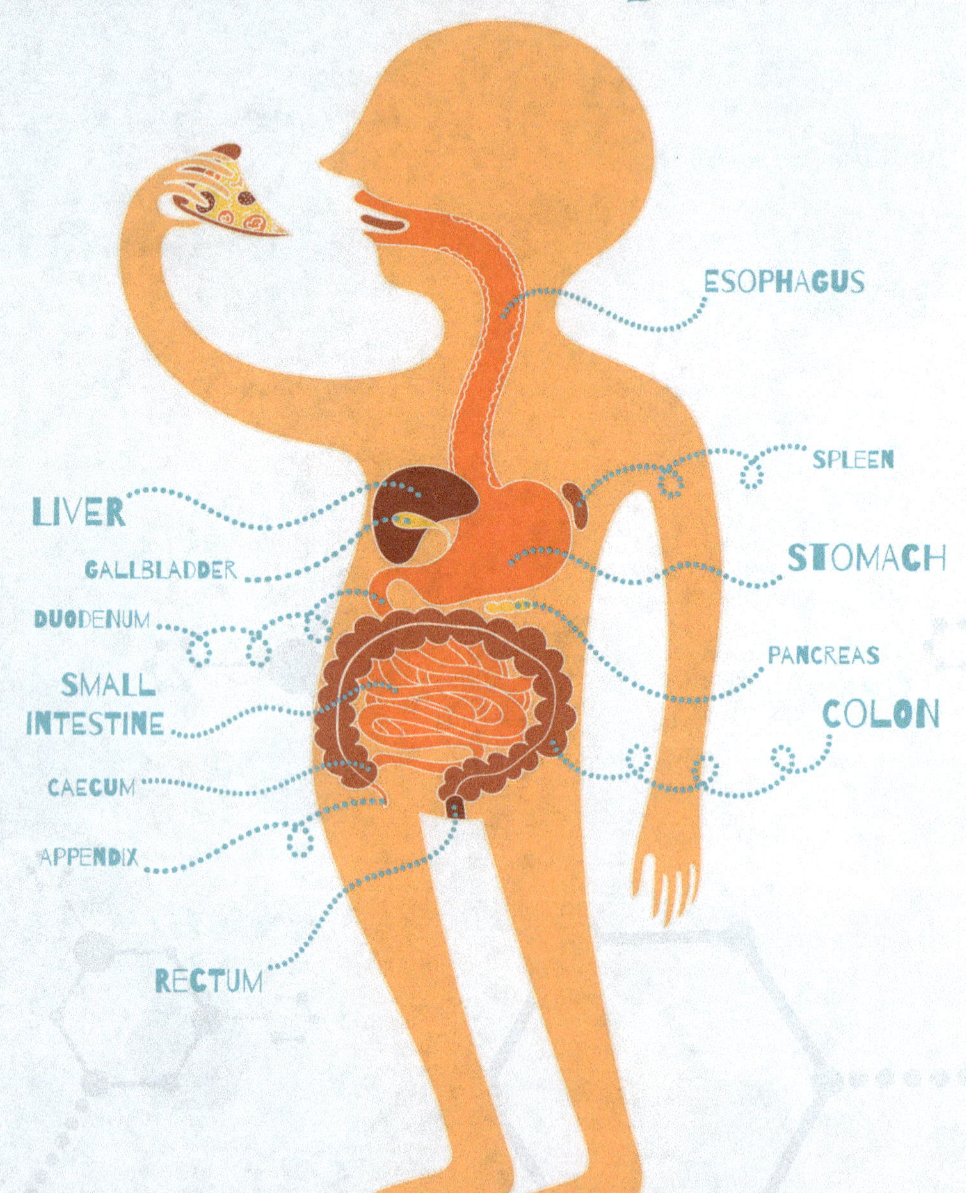

The urinary system utilizes the kidneys for filtering the blood and waste elimination, and includes the urethra, bladder, and kidneys.

The immune and lymphatic systems work together in protecting our body from diseases.

The reproductive system consists of sex organs which make it possible for people to have babies and is different for females and males.

The integumentary system helps in protecting our body from the outside world and consists of hair, skin, and nails.

Cartoon illustration of male and female urogenital system.

Urogenital system

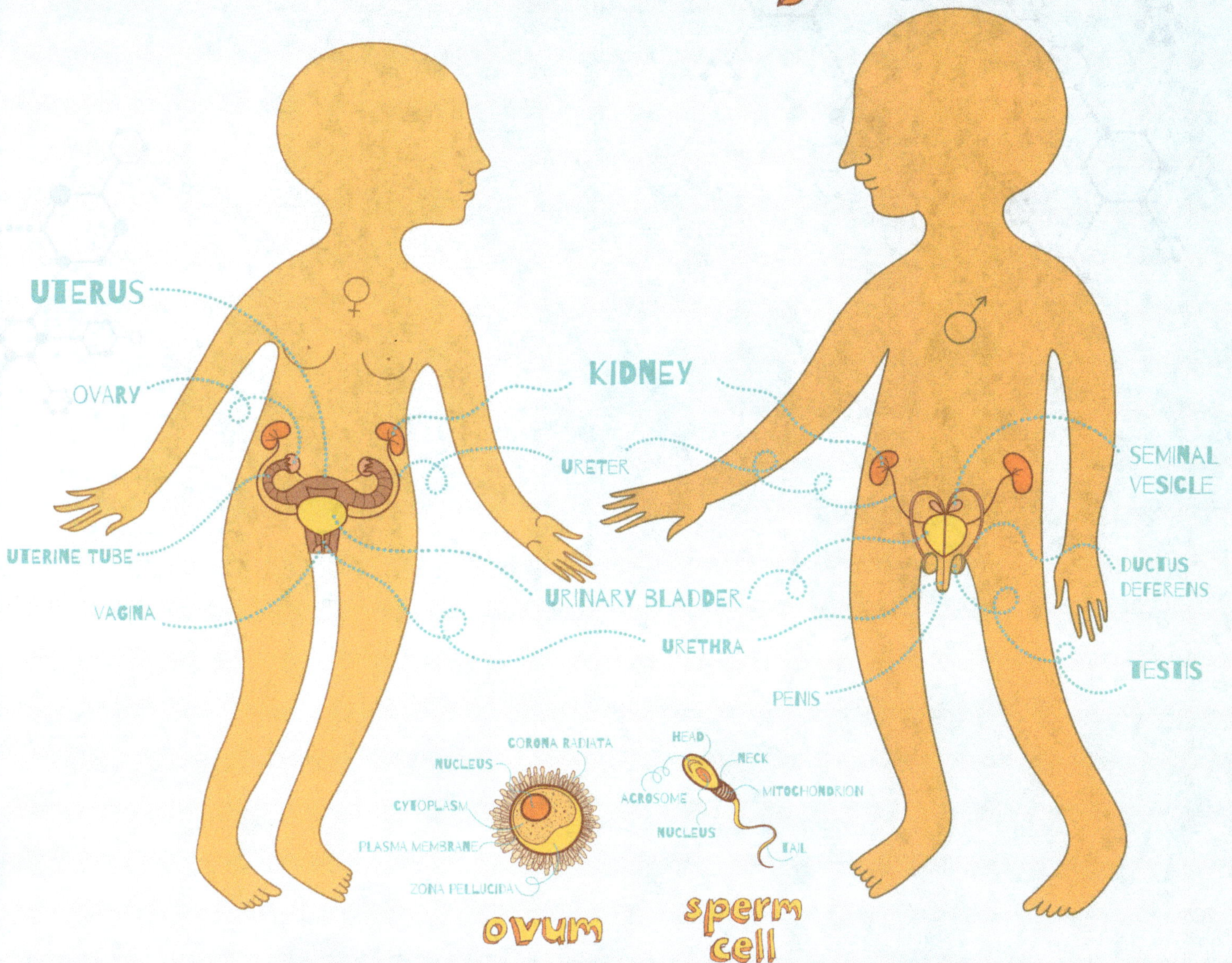

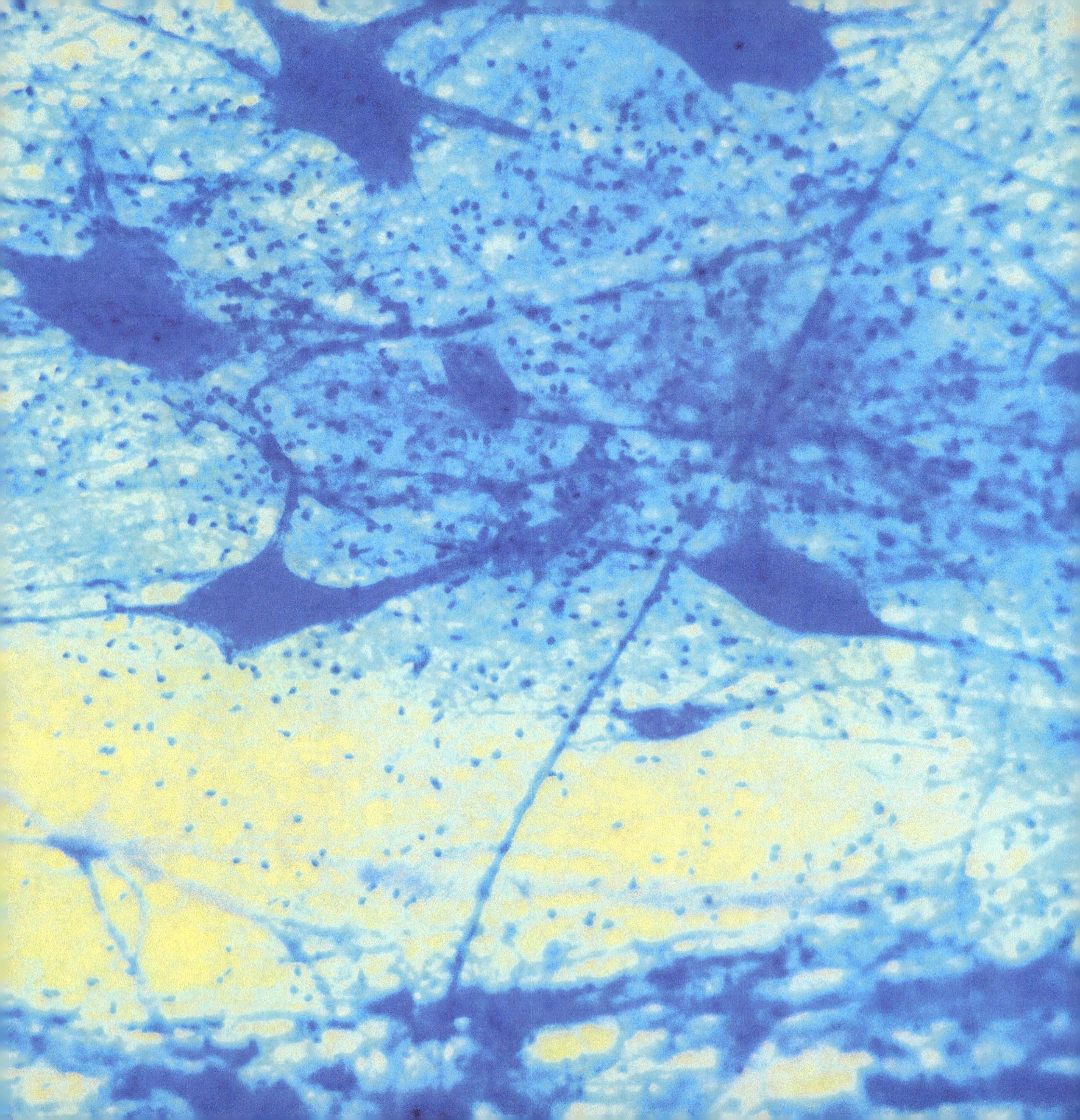

For additional information about the nervous system and the other parts of the human body you can go to the local library, research the internet, and ask questions of your teachers, family, and friends.

Nerve fibers: motor neurous- study with a large increase in the structural and functional nerve system.

Visit
BABY PROFESSOR
EDUCATION KIDS
www.BabyProfessorBooks.com
to download Free Baby Professor eBooks and view
our catalog of new and exciting Children's Books